Projects:
Skills and Strategies

Alma Williams

Pitman

PITMAN PUBLISHING LIMITED
128 Long Acre, London WC2E 9AN

Associated Companies
Pitman Publishing Pty Ltd, Melbourne
Pitman Publishing New Zealand Ltd, Wellington

© Alma Williams 1984

First published in Great Britain 1984

British Library Cataloguing in Publication Data
Williams, Alma
    Projects: skills and strategies
    1. Project method in teaching
    I. Title
    001.4′3   LB1027

All rights reserved. No part of this publication may be reproduced, stored in a retrieval system, or transmitted, in any form or by any means, electronic, mechanical, photocopying, recording and/or otherwise without the prior written permission of the publishers. This book may not be lent, resold, hired out or otherwise disposed of by way of trade in any form of binding or cover other than that in which it is published, without the prior consent of the publishers.

ISBN 0 273 02018 8

Text set in 10½ on 13 pt Times Roman
printed and bound in Great Britain
at The Pitman Press, Bath

Contents

Acknowledgments

1 Introduction 1
What is a project? 1
What sort of a project? 3
What's in a name? 4
Where did it all start? 5
What is the point of a project? 8
An echo from the past or a pointer to the future? 10

2 Constraints and challenges of the curriculum 12
How do children see their curriculum? 12
What are the needs of society? 12
What are the objectives of education? 13
What are the external constraints on the curriculum? 15
Does freedom of choice exist? 15
The challenge and the response: the project approach 18
Beating the system: conclusion 22

3 Plans and preparations 23
Choice and motivation – what's in a name? 23
Keyword suggestions 24
Ideas in action 25
Projects from problems 29
Projects from complaints 30
Generation and development of ideas 30
Brainstorming in action 32
Classification 33
Who is going to do what? 34
What needs to be done? 36
When is it all going to happen? 37
Where is the project going to be carried out? 38
Preparing the tools for planning 39
Finding out the facts 42

    Other sources of information   43
    Assembly of facts   44
    Problems in obtaining information   45
    Storage and retrieval of project information   49
    The need to know   51

4 Skills and strategies   52
    Carrying out a survey   53
    Designing a questionnaire – asking the right questions   58
    Asking and interviewing   70
    Testing and research   78
    Taste testing   87
    Simple scientific tests   92
    Investigating and inquiring   94
    Giving guidelines: stimulus materials   108

5 Presenting the results of a project   139
    Projectors in action   139
    What sort of presentation?   142
    Writing a report   145
    Alternatives to words   150
    Revision   165
    Making the most of the results   165

6 Conclusions and reflections   177
    Summary of the problems   177
    Pros and cons of project based learning   181

Bibliography   183

Index   186

Acknowledgments

The author would like to express thanks to the following for their help and permission to reproduce material:

British Gas
Consumers' Association, London
Consumer Affairs Bureau of the Australian Capital Territories
Consumers' Association of Penang
Consumers' Institute, New Zealand
Consumers Union of the United States, Inc (1975 copyright)
Dernières Nouvelles d'Alsace
Eastern Evening News, Norwich
Fred Boggis and CERES
International Organisation of Consumers' Unions
National Consumer Council
Population Concern
Queensland Consumer Affairs Bureau, Brisbane
Rowntree Mackintosh plc
Selangor Consumers' Association, Kuala Lumpur
Times Newspapers Limited
The Life Offices Association & Associated Scottish Life Offices, London & Edinburgh

Many other people – children, students, friends and family – have been involved in this book. I would also like to thank UNESCO, the Asia–Pacific Institute for Broadcasting Development and the Economic and Social Committee of the EEC. In addition, I single out Marylin Sludd, formerly at the CA, Raymond Ryba and Stephen Hodkinson of the 14–16 Economics Project, John Tulk from Wales, Liz French and Stephanie Sharpel from South Australia, Bishan Singh from Malaysia, Ophelia Cheung from Hong Kong and Arvind Deshpande from India. Finally, I thank my typist, Leslie Howlett, and my family for their support: my husband Michael, my sister Hilary Ball and my daughter Sheila, who has acted as my research assistant.

AW

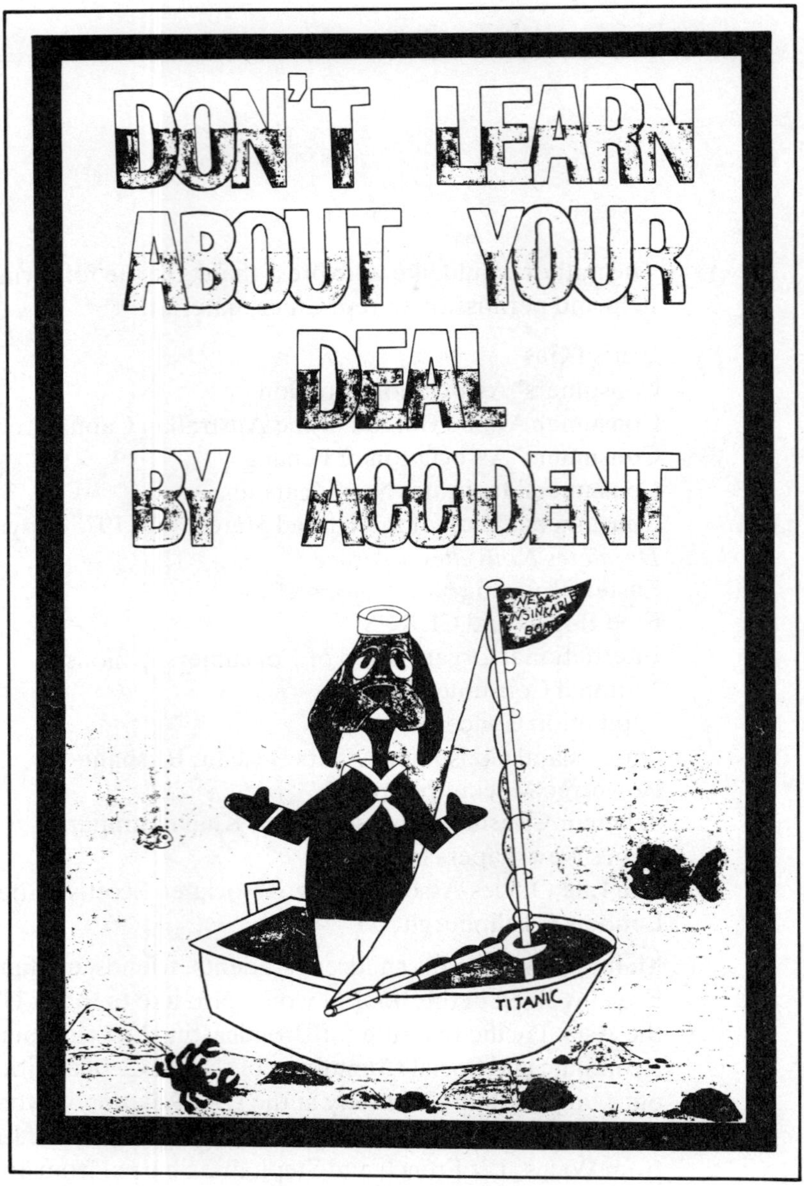
DON'T LEARN
ABOUT YOUR
DEAL
BY ACCIDENT
TITANIC

1 Introduction

What is a project?

'It's lots of bits of file paper with your work on and your charts and things that you often go and lose before you have to give them in.'

'It's what we were always having to do at the primary school – a sort of topic really.'

'It's what Miss says we've got to do in social studies for our CSE exam.'

'It's when we work together in groups and go out sometimes and find things out for ourselves.'

'It's looking things up in lots of different books about the same subject and copying them down.'

'Finding things out is great, but I don't like writing them down. Drawing's all right and making things is fine. Do we *have* to write?'

'It's thinking for ourselves about things that matter to us. Miss doesn't mind much if we don't agree with her.'

'It's learning to work with other people and do things for them.'

These were some of the comments made by a group of fourteen-year-old students in a mixed ability school in Hertfordshire who were doing projects for social studies. A similar discussion took place at a technical high school for girls in Jamaica, where British examination traditions have now disappeared, giving way to a more relevant system (Caribbean Examinations Council (CXC)) which emphasises the needs for commerce and social studies in a developing country. How did these girls in Kingston see project work? Did their views coincide with those of the British pupils? Their language was more orthodox and more careful, and their views linked to a study of tourism that they too were doing in social studies for the CXC exam.

'We find out answers for ourselves – we consult books and

newspapers and ask our grandparents what life used to be like under the British.'

'We study things and we think about them, and we don't have to learn by heart so much.'

'It's knowing the right questions to ask that's important because it shows you the problems; but there isn't always an answer.'

'It's learning to find out how *we* can help to solve problems, how we can make people want to come to our island and spend their money.'

'It's learning to make comparisons for ourselves – what has land drainage done to the people of Ochos Rios in the last ten years?'

'It's learning to understand charts and graphs, and the ways in which you can be misled by things in papers and magazines.'

None of these comments is complete in itself, but all have some element of truth in them, sometimes undesirable truth. Even teachers when put to the test find it hard to define a project, apart from relating it to 'learning by doing' or to some form of discovery or structured learning. Professional doubt and lack of confidence over definition are endorsed by the National Library's statement[1] that 'it was unusual to encounter any formal instruction for pupils in how to do a project.' Even in higher education 'only a few entrants have much experience of discovery methods in secondary school, and too many have been crammed with facts in order to pass examinations. A high proportion of students reach the tertiary stage without having been required to show any great ability towards independent learning situations.'[2] Since student ignorance is a measure of teaching methods, it is not surprising that a mature teacher of business studies on a 'Cert Ed' course (Certificate of Education (further and higher education)) at Middlesex Polytechnic should voice the opinion that she didn't really know but that she 'might have done a project once' but wasn't sure because she didn't know what was involved. So what can we accept as a useful, semi-official, well tried definition of a project? In 1973 C V Good wrote: 'It is a significant practical unit of activity having educational value and aimed at one or more definite goals of understanding; it involves investigation and solution of problems and, frequently, the use and manipulation of physical materials; planned and carried to completion by the pupils and teacher in a natural "real-life" manner.'[3] There is little reason to change this definition, though different kinds of project will need a different emphasis.

Looking back at the students' comments we can combine and

1 1979 survey of 24 comprehensive schools in Cheshire and Nottinghamshire

2 *Project Orientation in Higher Education*, ed M Cornwall & F Schmithals, Brighton Polytechnic & University Teaching Methods Unit, University of London, 1976, p. 128, see also p 68

3 Good C V, *Dictionary of Education*, McGraw Hill, New York, 1973

expand them into an itemised statement of expectations from projects, which follows on from Good's definition:

- some kind of positive action is involved
- some kind of organisation and structure is needed – self-discipline, group discipline, teacher imposed (even exam related) discipline
- some kind of end product (even if you do go and lose it before the end of the academic year) is required. This will often be a report, though it could be a drawing, a design, a recording, a computer program or a pilot product
- a project often involves the solution of a problem – like getting tourists to go to downtown Kingston – and it sometimes shows that the original problem is not the important one
- a project is not necessarily a lone activity: it is something that can be done in a group with each member contributing according to interest and ability
- learning initiatives are in the hands of the students, under their control
- teachers are advisory, a useful 'resource' material. They keep students on the right lines, or even allow them to go right off the lines if the educational objective is worth while
- projects are relevant to the needs and interests of the students and the society they grow up in

What sort of a project?

Is it in fact possible to produce a kind of identikit picture of a project? A look at projects in various parts of the world suggests that there are two main trends. In the first, which appears in more authoritarian systems, students concentrate on fact finding, which can be carried out with the classroom as a base; in the second students find out for themselves, using information only as a springboard for action.

In the first kind the teacher presents the subject, often as a problem relating to a current issue of a fairly general kind – the need for nuclear power, the relationship between word processors and potential unemployment for women, the achievement of industrial democracy at work, the implications of reducing lead in petrol, the desirability of controls over the content of television programmes. The problems underlying these subjects are usually of the type 'which course of action is right?' rather than 'which hypothesis is true?' And the main purpose of this kind of project is to achieve a better understanding. This may well mean that students tend to limit themselves to collecting more and better arguments to support their original views (always supposing that they are the sort of students who actually are thoughtful enough to have views). Unfortunately, this type of project does not normally encourage students to plan and perform experiments, carry out surveys, interpret results or test hypotheses. More often than not, it does result in vast screeds of A4 copied from books and papers in the hope that the teacher will not be aware of an unfamiliar style. Schools and colleges tend to push pupils in the direction of this kind of project for three main reasons: it is relatively easy to compile a register of topics based on a syllabus, to control and supervise output, and to keep within the confines of the classroom.

The second kind of project is a true learning-by-doing activity. Here students are given, or better still propose, a subject or problem for themselves and plan a logical, hopefully imaginative, course of action or series of solutions. How can emergency contact with old people be maintained in rural areas? How can supermarkets cut down on their enormous losses through theft? What sort of help can be given to young mothers who have to go out to work? Such subjects, which do not necessarily have to appear as questions, are real and relevant, and make heavy demands on thinking and evaluative skills. The answers are generally to be found not in other people's books but rather in the local community: emergency contact, for example, is defined in relation to a particular group of people living in a *named* village whose needs are analysed and evaluated. This kind of project can also include problem solving and design. How can the Qwerty keyboard be reformed? How can a pushchair be designed so that it is safe, stable and still has the capacity to carry large loads of shopping? How can a teaching aid be devised to teach handicapped people to tie their own shoelaces? There may be several courses of action which can be weighed one against the other, with reasons not all having the same weighting. There may indeed be no answer or solution at all in the end, but it is important for students to identify and accept failures and shortcomings as an essential part of a project. They will need to be reassured that in examination assessment a logical, well documented progression towards failure to find a solution does not imply inadequacy or incompetence, but it is hard to put over this message. It is demoralising – and it's life.

It is this second kind of project on which most guidance is needed and therefore most guidance given in this book.

What's in a name?

So far there has been the assumption that a project – a word which is now part of traditional educational jargon – is an active investigative ingredient in learning. It is also a word which is applied to inquiries, national or local, which emphasise research action and the need for an end product. In Britain, the Schools Council was a great producer of projects – on mathematics for the majority, moral education, the humanities curriculum, for example – and the Economics Association is involved in a wide ranging project on current economics and commerce courses, funded by the European Economic Community. Other organisations outside education, from the Marriage Guidance Council to the National Playing Fields Association, use the word. So do successive government programmes for unemployed young people. The Manpower Services Commission has begun a series of relevant, basic schemes: in one of these, twelve sixteen-year-old boys with not one O level pass among them actually made a two seater plane, learning skills on the job. Some organisations employ project officers (POs): the British Consumers' Association has POs, each in charge of a particular investigation or comparative test – on cars, carpets or kettles, building societies, banks or burglar alarms. Internationally, the World Health Organisation is sponsoring an expensive long term project to provide supplies of pure water through wells and pumps to large numbers of villages in developing countries. UNESCO has a low cost, short term project to teach two girls in the village of Induri in Maharashtra to learn about food and nutrition, health and hygiene; this is one of UNESCO's very smallest projects, but it is a *pilot* project which can be imitated and adapted for other villages. So, organisations of all kinds – charitable, commercial, financial and technological as well as educational – are involved in carrying out projects where the keywords are action and achievement based on research, investigation and the acquisition of skills. The difference between such projects and those in school or college, in Duke of Edinburgh Award schemes or Scout and Guide training, is really one of scale alone.

Where did it all start?

The Consumers' Association's staff, as well as students, would no doubt find it amusing to be called 'projectors', but this is the word Jonathan Swift used in the early eighteenth century in *Gulliver's Travels* to describe anyone involved in what he called 'speculative learning'. Gulliver says of himself, when accepting an invitation to inspect the Academy of Projectors at Lagado, 'I am a great admirer of projects and a person of much curiosity and easy belief . . . for I had myself been a sort of projector in my younger days.' Expurgated school editions of *Gulliver's Travels* mention only the most decorous projects, passing over the 'operation to reduce human excrement to its original food, by separating the several parts, removing the tincture it receives from the gall, making the odour exhale, and scrumming off the saliva.' But Swift sees the professors of the Academy as the arch-organisers of projects: to extract sunbeams out of cucumbers in five hundred rooms in which 'every room hath in it one or more projectors'; to mix colours for painters that could be distinguished by feeling or smelling; or to feed coloured flies to spiders in order to produce coloured silk instead of natural webs. The role of the pupils is, however, that of awe struck admirers rather than of active participants.

Moving on in time and place from Swift's original contribution, we find it is John Dewey who has the most right to lay claim to the project as an American inspiration and invention. Dewey's contribution to education was to deplore previous emphasis on cramming children with facts and demanding large amounts of learning by heart without much understanding – and testing what had been absorbed, if indeed anything at all. He believed in what he called 'the problem method of teaching', which required active involvement from students who had a new freedom to suggest their own problems and their own learning situations. He was convinced of the importance of relevance, seeing education as a present need rather than as 'preparation for a remote future'. This concept is very much in keeping with the philosophy behind the Nordic project of the late 1970s and early 1980s, a Scandinavian idea for educating children as consumers. In this, content is in line with current interests: so twelve-year-olds don't learn about tax systems or which washing machine they ought to choose, but about food, hobbies, sport, pets and pop music and the criteria for relevant choice and decision making.

Dewey's ideas spread across America during the 1920s. They were conceived and developed for *children* in the belief that even at an early stage they could accept more self-responsibility for learning than previous strict and rigid disciplines had allowed them. It is interesting that students in higher education were not his first targets for project based learning.

His ideas began to be incoporated into school systems in various other advanced countries. In Britain, in due course, the ideas received a boost from the setting up of the Nuffield Foundation, with its central philosophy of allowing children the freedom to make their own discoveries and think for themselves, to understand what they learn instead of routinely repeating mysterious drills. Generations of children later, Nuffield's ideas and ideals are not substantially challenged; the guides it published are still invaluable sources of suggestions for classroom activities and useful guidance on curriculum development. Perhaps the most important thing the Foundation achieved was to draw international attention to a new philosophy of primary education. It is largely thanks to Nuffield that parents for the last twenty years have been pestered by their offspring for help with their 'topic', and persuaded by door-to-door encyclopaedia salesmen that they had just the thing to help their child 'get on in life'. A contemporary quote from *Which?*, the magazine of the Consumers' Association, in January 1964: 'A neatly dressed young man walks into your messy kitchen, sits down and begins reading aloud from a book which will enable your children to be a success in life and meet distinguished people on equal terms.' Just the answer for responsible middle class parents beleaguered by topics. But the Nuffield approach did not remain confined to primary school activities: it moved into more advanced examination areas, with Nuffield maths and physics, for example, being accepted as alternatives to more traditional O level syllabuses. It was also accepted overseas in countries with a strong British connection through former colonialisation. The incorporation of Nuffield science, for example, into the timetables of some Malaysian schools began the development of logical, reasoned learning based on experiment rather than on being told. This was a revolution indeed in a country where, even now, in some Chinese-Malay schools, the word of the teacher is frequently regarded as unquestionably absolute and final.

The development of the Schools Council in Britain gave further impetus to project activity in schools and colleges after its establishment in 1964. In fact, the Nuffield Foundation was linked to the Schools Council in that it helped to fund the Midlands Mathematical Experiment, which was the forerunner of the Council's involvement in mathematical projects. Over the years the Council covered a range of subjects, or groups of subjects such as humanities. Its characteristic approach was learning based on pupils' own activities and environment, on a readiness to present concepts through concrete experience and example, on an element of discussion and oral work, on relevance to a student's interests and background, and frequently on a degree of curriculum integration with a thematic approach rather than one based on specialist disciplines.

Outside the formal education system other organisations have encouraged involvement in projects (see chapter 5), often on a one-off basis. The Royal Society for the Prevention of Accidents celebrated the silver jubilee of its Home Safety Division in 1982 and initiated safety projects. The Consumers' Association commemorated its twenty-first birthday in 1979 with a project competition for schools where the winning entries were televised on 'Money go round', and with an investigation by students into facilities for young children in hospital.

It is important to note the intervention of broadcasting in these projects. For a long time projects have been part of schools' broadcasting in Britain; as long ago as 1974 the Independent Broadcasting Authority was producing 'Decision' with teachers' notes and student support materials for projects on road planning, housing, shopping in hypermarkets, buying a car, and the Morecambe Bay barrage. But the media also encourage *activity through entertainment* in events such as 'Young scientist of the year awards', 'The great egg race', and 'Now get out of that', and through the competitions that 'Blue Peter' organises for younger viewers.

In view of this background it is hard to accept that many teachers still do not know how to go about organising a project. 'I did one once' said one of the 'Cert Ed' teachers on the Middlesex Polytechnic course, 'but it was a very bad one.' She taught commerce, but there are many teachers of other subjects in the same situation but perhaps less honest.

What is the point of a project?

Since, in spite of general ignorance and misgivings, so much attention is paid to projects, what have they to offer both to those who learn and those who teach, and those who in their wisdom work together? Obviously, they have to fulfil the generally accepted aims and objectives of education: in cynical terms they contribute towards the collection of the right pieces of paper with the highest possible grades, in order to satisfy the demands of parents and employers and achieve the fulfilment of teachers. At the same time projects can provide what Sir Alex Smith, former chairman of the Schools Council, called 'education for capability', a slogan which has now been taken up and developed by the Royal Society of Arts in a new sponsorship scheme. 'Education for capability' has the reality and the relevance sought by students, particularly those less able and less well motivated. 'What's the point of it, Miss?' is not an infrequent wail in current classrooms, particularly in areas of high unemployment.

So what has a project to offer that other forms of learning don't provide?

- It can give students the chance to develop basic skills and to *learn* in a relevant and often personal context. Ian did a comparison of maps in geography because he was a keen cyclist – and he learnt to read in the process and to tell his left hand from his right. In due course and after much effort he produced a comprehensive, accurate, comparative study of different editions. 'St Mary's didn't ought to be on that side of the road.' And it didn't!

- It can lead to an understanding that in the long term it is the process which counts rather than the product. In other words, in terms of learning for life, or capability, it is the skills that are important – *how* to communicate, to organise, to plan, to decide on the basis of fact, to collect information and evaluate it, and to present findings; then on to affective and social skills such as *how* to work together, to accept failure and the fact that failure is often relative, to develop self-confidence, independence and resourcefulness.

- It fits in with the existing educational traditions of many countries with western backgrounds. It adds to the 'telling and teaching' in the school leaver's letter quoted in chapter 2, the special significance of finding out. Facts are fleeting, but finding out – knowing how and why – is memorable when you do it for yourself. Even adults remember well chosen, appropriate projects. 'Do you remember that day we did Peter's dog?', said one full grown man with a small child tugging at his anorak (see chapter 4). For more than ten years Tom had remembered an investigation carried out in social studies into the cost of keeping a pet and the responsibility of having one. 'A pity I didn't realise it was the same thing with babies. I'll know better for the next one.' The lesson was only half successful: Tom had shown inability to adapt general principles to particular circumstances.

- It provides the satisfaction of a finished product which can be not only of personal but also of communal benefit. This 'product' may be a written report revealing defects in the local telephone system, or it may be the prototype of a new product such as a nonslip skirt or trouser hanger.

- It can, under certain circumstances, allow students to choose for themselves what they are going to work on. June did an investigation into diabetic products and their alternatives, because she had a strong sense of personal responsibility in a one parent family where her mother was a newly discovered and resentful diabetic.

- It can provide the chance for students to work together as a team, with each member contributing according to ability, and where collaboration can mean the difference between success and failure. Under pressure in a group, students can achieve things they never imagined possible.

- It demands participation, action and involvement – finding out whether the cycle sheds could cope with the expected increase in numbers of bikes when bus prices went up again, whether a cafeteria with individually priced items would be more popular than the flat rate conventional school dinner.

- It gives freedom from the constraints of a traditional exam paper. Time and place are no obstacle to a motivated student, and there isn't the tyranny of trying to recall facts frenetically crammed in the final moments. The aim of a project is not to test memory, but to allow students to collect their own ideas and examples, to work them out at their own speed, and to build up their own concepts at their own pace, proceeding with better luck than Tom from principle to particular.
- It ties in classroom work with community benefit. Steve, Andy and Marilyn did not like foreigners, yet they grudgingly started to help renovate two houses provided for Vietnamese refugees by the local authority. First they worked out costs, then painted, decorated and renovated old furniture, and ended with a curious but enthusiastic welcome for the newcomers. 'They aren't much different from us, really, but their English isn't half funny.'

An echo from the past or a pointer to the future?

There are fashions in educational jargon, with current – and quite sensible – international in-words including both 'life skills' and 'the world of work'. There are also fashions in teaching techniques, such as invidualised learning (which at its simplest means using an 'own pace' work card, at its most complex a computer program) and the use of case histories. In a sense, projects are old fashioned in that we can quote Swift on the subject although he wrote more than two centuries ago; the reality of definition is, however, that projects are all embracing and supremely adaptable to changing times and circumstances. Action is at the heart of any project, whether you want to extract sunshine stored up in cucumbers, design a solar powered oven for use in hot deserts, or find out how many public buildings have entrances wide enough for wheelchairs. Projectors in the final decades of the twentieth century can use the word 'project' in its broad, generic sense, adding to it and developing it as new methods of investigative learning become available and acceptable. Life as a projector is only just beginning in this age of new technology. For 'project orientation is not a passing educational fad but an important method that will have to be developed further in its many different manifestations.'[3] And as the 'Cert Ed' teachers on the Middlesex Polytechnic course concluded: 'A project is not a replacement of but a supplement to existing methods.'

[3] *Project Orientation in Higher Education*, ed M. Cornwall & F Schmithals, Brighton Polytechnic & University Teaching Methods Unit, University of London, 1976.

The practical implementation of a project

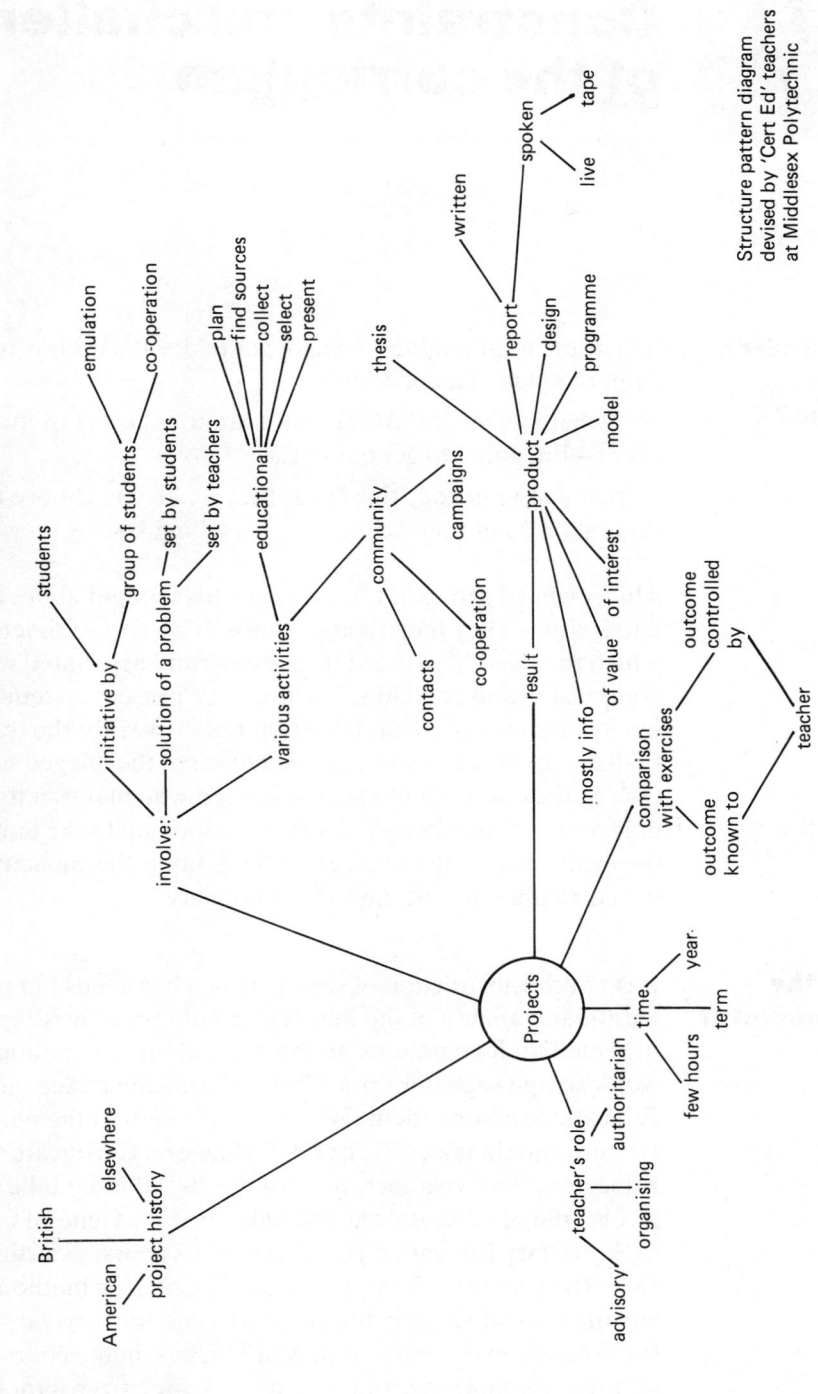

Projects

- **involve:**
  - **initiative by**
    - students
    - group of students — emulation
    - set by students — co-operation
    - set by teachers
  - **solution of a problem**
  - **various activities**
    - educational
      - plan
      - find sources
      - collect
      - select
      - present
    - community
      - contacts
      - co-operation
      - campaigns
    - product
      - thesis
      - report
        - written
        - spoken
          - live
          - tape
      - design
      - programme
      - model
      - of interest
      - of value
- **result**
  - mostly info
  - comparison with exercises
    - outcome controlled by teacher
    - outcome known to teacher
- **time**
  - year
  - term
  - few hours
- **teacher's role**
  - authoritarian
  - organising
  - advisory
- **project history**
  - British
  - American
  - elsewhere

Structure pattern diagram devised by 'Cert Ed' teachers at Middlesex Polytechnic

11

2 Constraints and challenges of the curriculum

How do children see their curriculum?

'It's a sort of timetable we've all got to do. It's useless really – I'd rather help my Dad in the shop.'

'It's what you've got to do if you want to take any of them exams. I don't – I'm going to get out at Easter.'

'When you're in your third year they make you choose things to do, only it's not really choosing, it's telling.'

This is what a group of fifteen-year-olds thought about the curriculum. They had a rough idea – 'It's a sort of timetable' – which they tied in with external exams and associated with compulsion and coercion. For them the present system is irrelevant, an understandable point of view since the traditional British scheme has been designed to serve the alleged needs of the few, of the one student in every sixteen who makes it to the university. 'While people continue to look up to the universities, they will not give the teachers in the schools the capacity to alter the curriculum to suit the needs of society.'[1]

[1] Brian Pimm, Head of Erith School, Kent, *Education for Capability Conference*, Royal Society of Arts, 1982

What are the needs of society?

It is not the abstraction of society which has needs but the identifiable reality of the Peters and Bobs and Chrissies who provided their comments on the curriculum – even though they won't scrape together three CSEs (Certificate of Secondary Education) among them. What are the needs of the million in Britain who do take CSE or GCE (General Certificate of Education) O levels each year, of the 300 000 who take GCE A levels, and of all those who will take the new General Certificate of Secondary Education (GCSE) with its courses starting in 1986? Does the present system, either in content or in method, prepare any of them adequately for life and living, for survival on the dole, for several job changes – if they are lucky – in the course of a lifetime, for marriage and parenthood, for citizenship, for increased leisure, and for a rapidly changing technology? It was an American school leaver who wrote the following letter complaining about the *content* of education, but similar accusations appear in British magazines:

'I want to know why you and your teachers did not tell and teach about life and the hard, critically practical world. I wish I had been taught more about family relationships, child care, getting along with people, interpreting the news, paying off a mortgage, household mechanics, politics, local government, the chemistry of food, carpentry, how to budget, the value of insurance, how to figure interest when borrowing money and paying it back in small instalments, how to detect shoddy goods, how to grow a garden, how to paint a house, how to get a job, how to be thrifty, how to resist high pressure salesmanship, how to buy economically and intelligently, the danger of instalment buying.'

And a British student protests about the *methods* imposed by exam boards:

'The exams are a marathon of recall, and it is soon impressed upon one that the bloodthirsty examiners are after facts, facts and true facts. In the land of the pink exam paper the elephant's memory is king.'[2]

2 Bruce Railton, *The Guardian*, 10 May 1983

What are the objectives of education?

Condemnation also comes from a much higher – and European – level in the final report on consumer education in schools produced by the Council of Europe for its member states:

'The primary objective of school education is to give pupils a general education and prepare them to play an active and enlightened role in society. In this respect the present situation is unsatisfactory since schools pay too little attention to the problems with which the individual will be faced in daily life.'

This report provoked a quick and positive Scandinavian reaction: four countries – Norway, Sweden, Denmark and Finland – cooperated in the Nordic project, mentioned in chapter 1, to find out the real needs of children both now and in the future. Governments, educators, class teachers and consumer organisations worked together to establish a structured, continuing, compulsory and essentially 'active' syllabus after much experiment, monitoring and evaluation. But in general, as the economic recession in Europe has grown worse, there has been little progress in changing the curriculum to suit 'the needs of society', and virtually no attempt, even with 9 million unemployed young people in European Economic Community countries, to replace the general concept of work with that of meaningful activity defined with dignity. In Britain:

'The obsession with a narrow academic achievement has become ever more intense. . . . With jobs increasingly hard to come by, parents, pupils and employers are demanding more and more paper qualifications. As a result, anything which is not strictly relevant to the examination syllabus – still largely made up of traditional academic subjects – is being progressively squeezed out of the school curriculum. This is about the worst possible direction in which education could be moving. It is true that a minority of our children . . . need a first rate academic education. It is also true that every child needs a thorough schooling in the basic skills of literacy and numeracy. But not for many children, perhaps the majority, for whom conventional academic qualifications designed to lead to conventional employment are irrelevant to the world in which they will live.

It is now surely becoming clear – although few politicians accept it – that western economies, and Britain's in particular, will not in the foreseeable future be able to provide full employment in the sense we have known it for the last 150 years or so.

The pattern of activity for many is likely to be a mixture of self-sufficiency, exchange and barter of goods and services, and cultural and leisure pursuits, some of it paid, some unpaid.

Schools should be preparing and equipping their pupils for this trend towards more diverse activity. Yet how many are offering as a central feature of the curriculum such a basic and important skill as gardening – a subject which would promote self-sufficiency?'[3]

3 Ian Bradley, Let's teach our children to live, *The Times*, 14 February 1983

Nevertheless, in Britain, as in many other countries, this is a time of deliberation about the direction of education, a time for changes – proposed, rejected, reshaped – with a new unified exam at 16+ (the GCSE) starting in 1988, using new content and new methods. There is an undoubted need for a change in public attitudes and expectations. When the reorganisation of education in Australia was the subject of general debate, parents were asked in a national opinion poll what they wanted their children to learn at school. Ninety-four per cent of them wanted consumer studies to be taught (though there is a suspicion that they saw this as a kind of single dose immunisation against rip-offs and 'krook' purchases rather than a continuing life long process). How would British parents, and indeed teachers, react in a similar poll?

Would examination success and getting a good job, or indeed any job at all, still be singled out as the foremost aims of education?

What are the external constraints on the curriculum?

In Britain, public attitudes have been 'conditioned' through the domination of the universities that is maintained by the examination boards. At present there are two entirely separate *external* examining systems for schools, which must seem very strange to the rest of Europe where exams at 16+ are internal arrangements. There are twenty-two boards in England and Wales: eight of them (some of them recognised overseas) deal with GCE at O and A levels, and fourteen with CSE. In spite of the technical autonomy of schools, it is these examination boards which, under the sway of the universities, set out to provide guidelines and a generally accepted standard for students and staff, parents and employers. But they duplicate and jumble up a whole range of different but not dissimilar types of test instead of allocating specific related subjects in graded steps to particular boards. Under present conditions it is they who affect and control the content of courses in secondary schools and colleges of further education. Take consumer education, for example, as a general theme. Though in June 1981 there were fifty-nine different subjects all containing elements of consumer education (the main ones appear in the chart on page 16 for checking theme with subject), ranging from home economics to history, from social studies to science, there is considerable variability. Some boards, like the Oxford and Cambridge Schools Examination Board, don't offer home economics at all; others, like the Associated Examining Board (which now imaginatively combines its O level family economics with a popular radio programme) produce a substantial amount in a number of their syllabuses. Others contain consumer education in the text which they publish every year but don't actually get round to asking any questions. Some have very narrowly based questions, but a few do require projects or realistic problem solving, or involve the analysis of case histories.

Does freedom of choice exist?

Access and opportunity, denial and deprivation – these are the possibilities that such variability brings to pupils studying for external exams; and it is often simply luck of the draw whether there is a chance to take the subjects they need or want. This 'luck' depends on the boards that the school or college historically

Chart for checking the thematic approach

	art and design	business studies and commerce	child care	community studies	economics	environmental studies	English	geography	health education	history	home economics	languages	maths	religious education	science	social studies	others
Influences on consumer																	
needs and wants																	
values																	
goals																	
lifestyles																	
advertising																	
marketplace																	
society																	
economic system																	
Managing money																	
budgeting																	
banking																	
credit																	
insurance																	
taxation																	
savings																	
investment																	
Buying and using																	
food																	
clothing																	
housing																	
transport																	
household goods																	
services																	
leisure																	
Rights and responsibilities																	
marketplace																	
legislation																	
safety																	
environment																	

[4] Equal Opportunities Research Bulletin 6, *Gender and the Secondary School Curriculum*

uses, the subjects that a school with tight staffing ratios is able to offer, and on the options that the student makes at age fourteen. Was Peter right in saying 'it's not really choosing, it's telling'? The Equal Opportunities Commission[4] suggests that pupils generally felt they had made up their own minds, with their parents as the main influence. Nevertheless, such decisions are likely to have been pretty intensively guided, within the constraints of what the school can offer, through form filling, family discussion and general consultation. Obviously, Peter was sensitive to what he felt was pressure. The choice of abler students is restricted because they are directed into an early specialisation, penalised by being routed into O and A level courses rather than into CSE where most project based courses exist; others suffer quite simply from being the wrong sex. The Equal Opportunities Commission confirms that even in what it calls 'good practice schools' subjects could still be allocated by sex, with girls doing needlework and boys technical drawing.

The introduction of the General Certificate of Secondary Education will merge O levels and CSEs and will create a single system of examinations run by a much smaller number of boards responsible for syllabuses based on national criteria. Although it will bring long-awaited improvements, and even innovations, present problems meanwhile continue to affect schools.

The main limitations of choice exist, then, in the following areas, with teachers affected and directed as well as students:

- in the restrictions of tradition – of being tied to one or two exam boards which may not offer what is now needed either in method or in content

- in the guidelines, instructions and explanations printed in the text of the syllabus, which can vary from vague hints and straight lists of topics to be studied to practical help about assessment and the provision of bibliographies

- in the variability of the syllabuses

- in the option system, which forces students to specialise at an early age, with a sex bias still in operation

- in the assumption that questions are going to be set on the syllabus

- in the lack of reality and relevance of many syllabuses, which do not satisfy the needs of students of all abilities and both sexes

The challenge and the response: the project approach
Making the most of CSE

In the face of these difficulties, and the problems that are discussed in full in chapter 6, the only reasonable question to ask is: what can we do with what we've got?

Firstly, we can look at examination subjects and the kinds of teaching and testing that they require. Some of them already include a project as part of their syllabus, and if they don't . . .? The possibility here is to get rid of traditional allegiance, to take advantage of the variability it is so easy to condemn, and to move on to a different exam board. Alternatively, there are other organisations which offer acceptable qualifications, such as City and Guilds certificates. But even at a high academic level – A level physics, for example – a subject can be assessed partly on the basis of a project, and at a lower level there are plenty of opportunities to be taken advantage of in CSE.

The fourteen regional boards for CSE, set up in 1962 to have a much wider appeal than the GCE board, offer three different kinds of exams:

- *mode 1* – an external exam based on a syllabus prepared by teachers serving on subject panels
- *mode 2* – also an external exam, but based on a syllabus prepared by an individual school or group of schools
- *mode 3* – a different kind of exam, set and marked internally by teachers, but based on a syllabus submitted by a school or group of schools for approval and moderation by a particular board

It is mode 3, particularly in subjects like social studies, which gives an enthusiastic teacher the chance to include project work, relating it to the needs of students living in an area with its own special identity. Projects can be submitted in a variety of forms for assessment as part of the CSE exam, which also includes a written section consisting of multiple choice questions, and an oral on the general themes which the students have studied. In mode 3 it is possible for them not only to study child care theoretically but also to go out and work for an afternoon a week in a nursery, and to initiate an inquiry into local facilities for looking after small children; it is possible for them not only to accept other people's handicap as an unpleasant remoteness, but also to work in a mental hospital, to form relationships with patients, to learn bitterly about political realities when trade union officials object to them pushing dinner trolleys in the wards; it is possible for them to find out what other people think about the ridiculous anomalies of Sunday trading laws in England.

Even if they can't carry out in-depth studies, students can still work on smaller, clearly defined projects which can be tailored to fit a 40 minute period. Such a project might be a comparative study of instructions for use, for example. Can you understand them? Are they clear and logical? Is the design and layout helpful to the user? Are there adequate warnings when necessary? Such questions are equally relevant in woodwork or craft when applied to adhesives, in commerce and mathematics to calculators or computers, in home economics to sandwich makers, slow cookers or microwave ovens.

Such projects, developed in detail in chapter 4, concern 'the needs of society' and fulfil the relevant, realistic requirements of students both in content and in method. 'I want to know why you and your teachers did not tell and teach about life and the hard, critically practical world' – the two students quoted at the beginning of this chapter would not have uttered the same reproaches at the end of a well organised, project based CSE course.

Working within compulsion

Many countries, though not Britain, have a core curriculum of essential subjects which students are obliged to study. In India, for example, the school leaving certificate is based on the total number of marks students get in maths, science, language and social studies, with language subdivided into Hindi, English and the state language, and with social studies subdivided into history, geography and civics. Compulsion in itself is not an obstacle to project work, since in those countries where it exists the range of subjects includes all those where there are already opportunities for active, investigative learning. The key question is whether these opportunities can be seized. Certainly it is likely that most projects carried out will be of the first kind mentioned in chapter 1, based on collecting and evaluating existing information, but here too moves can be made to extend the scope and link the school with both the community and 'the world of work'. This is the intention of Mrs Gandhi in introducing 'socially useful and economically productive classes' into secondary school syllabuses in India (see page 20).

The importance of influence and involvement

In spite of the constraints imposed by British universities and exam boards, Her Majesty's Inspectorate, together with subject advisers and teachers, does have some say in formulating exam syllabuses at all levels. But it is in CSE courses that classroom teachers can have the greatest influence. All three modes have a considerable teacher input, but in mode 3 there is responsibility not only for designing the course and the way it will be taught but

Diagram designed for the South Indian state of Karnataka to show how existing compulsory subjects could incorporate consumer education.

Sectors (clockwise from top):
- **LANGUAGE** (Hindi, Kannada): Looking at advertising, packaging, labelling, promotion; communicating with people who cannot read; understanding instructions for use; warning; social significance of local radio; the press — *Communicating, using & understanding words*
- **Maths**: Budgeting; money lending; interest rates; insurance; saving money — *Using & interpreting figures*
- **History**: Marketing to a cash - barter inflation; dev. of legislation society; — *Learning facts*
- **SOCIAL STUDIES** (Geography): Local surveys - transport, water supply; facilities for the sick; national exp. patterns; rural communities — *finding things out, assessment*
- **SOCIAL STUDIES** (Civics): Problems of beggars; housing needs; social & medical services; democracy in action; subsistence
- **Science**: Detection & prevention; Detection & adulteration of food tests e.g. colour simple tests; ISI; qualities fastness; & properties of new materials — *Comparing measuring evaluating*
- **English**

Inner ring: BUYING / SERVICES / SELLING / GOODS — **YOU**

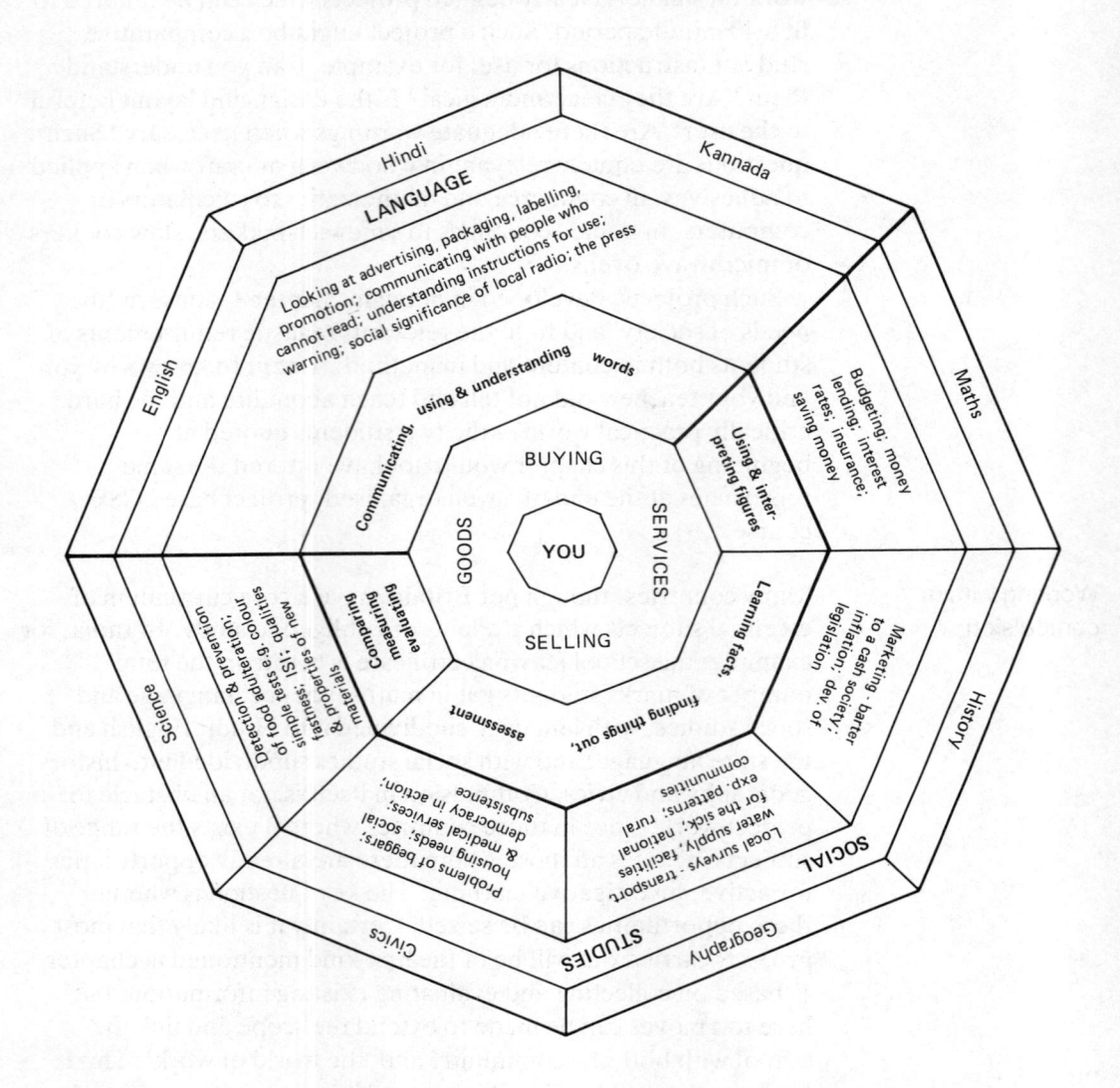

for marking and assessment as well. The system is normally for a department to draft its own syllabus in outline and in detail, incorporating items of special interests to students, and indicating particular techniques for teaching as well as suggestions for assessment; the draft is then sent to the appropriate exam board for approval. Once they accept the syllabus, it is up to the teachers to set and mark the papers each summer. With this degree of involvement possible, there is no reason to bewail the lack of opportunity for introducing projects as part of the package. Opportunities can be created.

Working informally

Many secondary schools now start their children off with a series of broad based subjects such as general, environmental or integrated studies, or introduce a programme of home economics for all during the first two years. It is then, before exam choices are made and pressures build up, that there is time for more unstructured opportunities in the timetable. Rural studies, for example, produces a project on the impact on community and consumers of the merging of small farms into large units – not just an academic exercise but the reality of the welly boot and the wet, wearisome actuality of finding out. Simultaneously but independently, two schools chose the same subject – one in East Anglia and the other in Alsace, the latter involving a survey of 700 farmers. A well run project is no child's play, and endurance is a useful attribute.

Alternatively, there are the opportunities offered by nonexamination courses, not only in Britain but in other countries too: France, for example, has introduced 'dix pour cent de temps libre' into a highly structured and compulsory curriculum. The problem is that, since such courses do not have the same status as an exam subject, they are often despised and badly attended unless there is some other kind of appeal. What are the criteria for success of nonexam courses? What do students think?

'If it's not any use I'll hop off.'
'Well, it must be different that's all.'
'We must actually *do* something.'
'They must let us get out.'
'It's got to be a surprise, like, so's we don't know what's coming next.'

All these demanding criteria can be met by a project suggested or self-selected with the students' needs and interests in mind, using a number of different techniques, well organised so that it is quite clear that this isn't a second best course just because there is no piece of paper at the end of it. The record survey reproduced in chapter 4 is a good example of a popular project. A chance remark to an adept class teacher can also trigger off an unscheduled project: the telephone kiosk survey in chapter 4 arose out of a spontaneous grumble that 'the telephone boxes on our estates are always out of order'; an epidemic of gimmicky mail order wristwatches that wouldn't work led on to an investigation of mail order in general; the eviction of an Indian boy and his family produced an inquiry into local housing and tenants' rights. Such projects can generate an unexpected enthusiasm which spills over into students' own time: the painting and decorating of

Vietnamese refugees' homes extended into weekends, and prowling round telephone boxes occupied evenings. A new set of problems appears – the need for school consent, parents' approval, and teachers' supervision, however casual – but at least apathy is no longer the enemy of action.

Beating the system: conclusion

In spite of controls, constraints and even compulsion, it is still possible to find diverse – and sometimes devious – ways of introducing some kind of inquiry or investigation into a large number of scheduled subjects. It is also possible to seek out opportunities outside this framework and form a link between school and community. As the Council of Europe says quite forcefully in its report: 'It's up to the teacher.' The purpose of this book is to enable the teacher to fulfil that function.

3 Plans and preparations

Choice and motivation – what's in a name?

'Safety's boring, Miss. Accidents is interesting.' A hand raised in polite but forceful protest. Many voices calling out in agreement. A class revolt? Safety appeared in the CSE mode 3 exam syllabus for social studies, but class 4b were not inspired by the idea of any project, group or individual, on safety. A quick flash of a thought, an instant reversal of attitude – they *had* got a point. Would it really matter to the East Anglia Examining Board whether it was accidents or safety that were studied? Either way the subject would be covered: one way reluctantly, the other enthusiastically.

Choice and motivation are closely linked but, within a formal exam syllabus or compulsory curriculum, choice can be restricted. Nevertheless, CSE mode 3 gives scope, and even within O and A level subjects the frequent vagueness of the syllabus – sometimes irritating for teachers seeking more practical guidance – can be used to advantage. Instructions for use, the retail trade, the health service, child care can appear as irrelevant abstractions, particularly to the 4bs of this world. But you can interpret such abstractions in such a way that introductions and briefing sessions start off with a lively, dramatic, relevant example, moving on from particular item to general aims and implications: a model plane hobby kit where you are told to glue the two halves of the fuselage together . . . and then fix the pilot inside; a shocking story from a local paper about cockroaches in a local café; a prescription form to fill in; a baby's rattle filled with lead shot; and so on. Nonexam subjects, those undertaken as in-depth studies in the gap between O level exams and the start of A level courses, the French system of ten per cent free time mentioned in chapter 2, all give you more scope for freedom of choice. So do awards and competitions with a given framework which is seldom inhibiting: the Hong Kong Consumer Council's demand for cartoons on consumer rights, for example, actually produced 2000 entries, and the British Consumers' Association's competition attracted a diversity of projects ranging from farming and livestock to soap, school meals, freedom of the press, the post office, transport and buying calculators.

Choice of subject, or at the very least consultation about it, marks the start of independent learning, a process in which students are deliberately given more and more freedom to make important decisions – and to have to come to terms with the consequences of an unwise or ill informed choice. The degree of choice depends on the ability, aptitude and attitude of those doing the projects: a diligent sixth former or group of sixth formers, with intentions of going on to higher education, will put less strain on a teacher than 4b, who demand their say in what they are going to do.

But what of the child who says 'I don't know what to do, Miss.' In order to survive you need a stockpile of useful keyword titles extracted from your syllabus – fortunately a basic one-off exercise with gradual additions – which you match in with your student's known interests. Tom's delight in reading *Exchange and Mart*, and in the sometimes dubious products he sent off for (like the furry knickers which were once delivered to him at school), was associated with a very successful commerce project on mail order, though right through to the conclusion he insisted that it was 'male' order. Such reluctant or deviant projectors have to be watched in case they sneakily do the same project for two different teachers of two different subjects. The suggestions which follow could have such overlaps, since they are on the whole equally applicable to business studies, economics, commerce, home economics, social studies and environmental studies. They are drawn from current syllabuses at all levels.

Keyword suggestions	advertising	food additives
	packaging	old age
	labelling	moonlighting
	product design and development	protectionism
		pets
	housing	food chains
	clothing	water
	conservation	mail order
	standards	pirating/counterfeiting
	fashion	adulteration
	pollution	safety
	environment	markets
	marketing and distribution	travel
	budgeting	tourism
	contracts	international trade

trade unions
food and nutrition
welfare services
drug abuse
wages and incomes
hazardous substances
impact of new technology
pesticides
community services
product safety
vandalism
credit and loans
exports and imports
insurance
investment
mass media communications
needs and wants
production and industry
saving
transport
supply and demand
government services
taxation
subsidies
free enterprise
nationalisation

social services
brand names
smoking
interdependence of nations
advice industries
European Economic
  Community
guarantees
how to complain
propaganda
censorship
sponsorship
leisure
production chain
purchasing methods
multinational corporations
repairs
do-it-yourself
consumer protection
health and safety
energy
alternative sources of energy
noise
problems of the disabled
factory farming
insulation

You can keep suggestions on index cards, add to them, comment on them, and record who is doing what. Or you can develop a more complex punchcard system, incorporating continuous assessment with easier retrieval of names and subjects.

Ideas in action

A very perplexed home economist sat gazing at the Cambridge A level syllabus for needlework. 'Informative labelling' she read out. 'What on earth does it mean in practical terms? What shall I do?' This is precisely the problem that the list of suggestions leaves still to be solved, especially in the case of interdisciplinary or wide ranging subjects. It is the problem of the Indian teachers who are faced with 'socially useful and economically productive subjects' to be incorporated into a fairly narrow, traditionally compulsory core curriculum. The home economist might have felt more confident in her own ability and more alert to the latent knowledge she undoubtedly possessed if she had had the

Labelling

following guidance, which is split up into general background information, suggested activities for students, and resource materials.[1]

[1] *Consumer Education: a Research Handbook for Teachers*, Consumers' Association, 1979

A label may:

- tell you how to use or care for something (for example, how to wash an acrylic sweater)
- warn you of the dangers of using or misusing a product or not following the instructions (for example, labels on medicines warning you not to exceed the stated dose)
- tell you that an article has been tested and approved (for example, the British Standards Institution kitemark)
- act as a point-of-sale advertisement (for example, illustrations on food packets)
- tell you what an item is made of (for example, the fibres in a carpet or the chemicals in an instant pudding)

A study of labelling could concentrate on any one of these approaches, or could be included as one aspect of a study of packaging or advertising.

In international terms, symbolic labelling is becoming increasingly important. However, symbols can be confusing. A *Which?* survey found that very few people understand the new EEC hazard warning symbols for dangerous substances, including household products such as caustic soda and paraffin.

Suggested activities for students

- Hold a brainstorming session and ask one student to write on the board all the different sorts of labels the class can think of. Collect examples of each sort and divide them into categories.
- Obtain the list of ingredients from packets of such products as Angel Delight, Coffeemate or Dream Topping. Read them to the rest of your class, without identifying the products, and ask them to guess what the products are. How do they react when you tell them the names of the products?
- Collect labels from empty cans of vegetables, soup packets and jam or marmalade jars. Look at the lists of ingredients and find out the meanings of all the words you don't understand.
- Have a look at articles of used clothing, household linens and pairs of shoes. Do they have labels? If so, what information do they give? How permanent are the labels? Does this matter?
- Imagine that you have had to do all the family's washing and ironing for the first time with no one to help and advise you.

Discuss what you would have to be careful about. How much help could you get from the labels (not just the labels on the clothes themselves)?
- A new series of international symbols which should make mopeds safer and easier to use has recently been introduced. Can you match up the words and symbols?

Upper beam	Engine ignition cut off
Fuel	Lower beam
Horn	Master lighting switch

- Devise a set of symbols which could be used internationally for the controls of a music centre.

A harassed male colleague sat looking at the Southern Exam Board's CSE business studies syllabus. Retail outlets? No time to think, no time to prepare adequately, but he did have a solution:

Retail outlets
(*Consumer Education: a Research Handbook for Teachers*, Consumers' Association, 1979)

You may not see as many butchers, bakers or candlestick makers in your local high street as you once would, but there is still an enormous variety of shops. There are specialist shops – greengrocers, electrical shops, chemists – and there are corner shops selling everything, sometimes at all hours, from newspapers to frozen meals. There are larger shops and stores – departmental, chain, cooperative etc. And there are ice cream vans and vending machines, mobile shops, milkmen and markets. Each provides its own version of consumer service and each has its advantages and disadvantages for the consumer.

All have been affected in some way by the shopping revolution which has taken place since the last war. Postwar labour shortages encouraged the development of self-service – quick, lower priced and impersonal – and created supermarkets. More recent preoccupation with prices is encouraging the growth of discount houses and cash and carry warehouses and making planners reconsider their opposition to out-of-town shopping centres and hypermarkets. And more retailers are choosing to sell own brand products, even among nonfood items, rather than manufacturers' brands.

When you have a choice of places from which to buy, then price, after sales service, delivery, credit, opening times, car parking facilities and distance away from your home all influence your decision. Buying in bulk requires estimation of needs, careful planning of budgets and consideration of storage problems. Market stalls can provide bargains as well as headaches if goods are not satisfactory and the stallholder has moved on.

Although shopping around is a bore for most people, it can be a necessary bore, as it is one of the few ways of exploiting the huge range of retail outlets in order to minimise the effect of inflation.

Suggested activities for students

- Carry out a survey to find out when (days and times) your parents do their shopping. Include regular food shopping and shopping for one-off items like clothes and furniture. Would they like to shop at other times? Are shops open at the times people need them? If not, why not?
- Draw a plan of your local shopping centre, marking in all the different shops. Are there too many of some and not enough of others? Do they cater for everybody's needs? Are there things you cannot buy there?
- Where can you buy things apart from the local shops? Is there a market? What about vending machines or the station bookstall? What about delivery men like the milkman and the baker? What are the special advantages of these ways of buying?
- Find the cheapest place in your area to buy *a* vegetables *b* torch batteries *c* tights *d* casette tapes. Are the cheapest places always the most convenient or sensible places in which you can shop? Or would the next cheapest place sometimes give you a better buy in the long run?
- The elderly or disabled, and mothers with small children, can find shopping very difficult – stairs, escalators, swing doors and lack of lifts all present problems. Are there any places in your area which offer special facilities for them?

Syllabus keywords

Sometimes the syllabus keywords (in italic) can be expanded, perhaps into questions, to form the basis for either an instant or a longer term project:

1. What sorts of anti*pollution* measures exist (e.g. emission control on vehicles), and how do they affect people both as individuals and as members of society? What still needs to be done?
2. What sorts of control exist in *advertising?* How do they work? Are they good enough or should more be done?
3. Is *consumer protection* by governments unfair to trade?
4. How much waste do we buy – *packaging*, paper, plastic and so on? What are the effects on the economy and the environment?

5 A new typewriter (*purchasing*) has to be bought for the office of:
- a small business
- a firm with a big export trade
- a self-employed person

Research the buying of a suitable model by considering the problems raised in each situation, by gathering information and by evaluating alternatives.

6 Are *branded goods* better than nonbranded? What do you mean by 'better'? Why are there so many brands? What are the differences? Are some made by the same company?

7 'I don't mind what you do as long as it doesn't hurt anyone else.' Consider ways in which individual behaviour can affect others both in financial and nonmaterial ways (e.g. shoplifting, *moonlighting*, travelling without a ticket).

8 Why were so many high rise blocks of flats built, and why aren't local authorities building them now? Interview people who live in them and find out what they like and dislike about them. What sorts of families particularly dislike them? (*housing*)

9 Collect proposal and claims forms from different *insurance* companies and complete them for real or imaginary risks or disasters. How easy is it? Do you fully understand the forms? Why is it vital to be absolutely truthful in your dealings with insurance companies?

10 Why is it important to *design* products with reuse, replacement parts and recycling in mind? Choose an existing product as an example and redesign it taking these needs into account.

You will need to remind students that these are not essay questions, and that each one is to contain evidence of some sort of investigation.

Projects from problems

A real problem – and design problems play more part here – can again provide an enthusiastic response because age is no bar to effective or feasible solutions:

- There are many more *old people* – over 75 – in the community now. How are they to spend their final years? How can they be cared for with dignity at a time when there is less money for state care?
- If door-to-door deliveries by *postmen* stop, we shall need to have some system of having our mail delivered to our gates.

Design a suitable, vandal proof domestic letter box for houses in a suburban area.
- Gas, electricity and water bills have a standing charge built in. Many people don't like this. How would you convince them that it is fair? Or can you think of an alternative? (*energy*)
- Ignorance of the *law* is no excuse – even a blind person is expected to be aware of the laws of the land. What can be done about the widespread ignorance of the law?
- *Protectionism* and industry – British textile and footwear workers want to keep their jobs, but consumers want the wider choice and lower price that comes with the jeans and jerseys from Korea and Hong Kong. How can the different points of view be accommodated?

Projects from complaints

This is a particularly useful ploy with academically 'turned-off' students who, in other capacities, are only too ready to grumble – albeit with certain justification – about the world they find themselves in. More often than not their complaints will contain the words 'always' or 'never'. Take their lament mildly at its face value – and let them set out to prove their point reasonably and responsibly. The first example (see chapter 4) is a case where the class in question, protesting to a teacher they trusted, did turn out to be right – if 'often' is substituted for 'always'.

'The telephone boxes are always out of order when we want to ring up our boyfriends.'

'That first class post is a waste of money. Your letters never get delivered the next day like they say they do.'

'Nobody likes that UHT milk. Them Frogs shouldn't be allowed to bring it into our country.'

'The films end at our cinema five minutes after the last bus has gone.'

'It's not fair. Why can't we travel on the bus half price all the time we're still at school?'

'It's not fair. We shouldn't have to pay that extra tax on sanitary towels. We don't buy them for fun and we could spend our money on better things.'

Generation and development of ideas

The subject has been chosen in general terms. With luck and tact it has now the support of participatory enthusiasm because of your efforts to take into account interests, relevance and democracy. But the subject has to spawn ideas. Class 4b had transformed safety (from the keyword list) into accidents but they had to be induced to move on from there. Fortunately, they – like many other rather reluctant learners – appreciated the use of techniques from business and management. The fact that brainstorming, critical path analysis and problem solving are recognised assets in industrial creativity and strategy can give them a status to students who have a certain touchiness about being talked down to. Brainstorming, for example, is useful for the generation and classification of ideas in the early stages of a project, and can guarantee – if you handle it properly – a response from even the most unwilling or shyest student (because it is cooperative rather than competitive). The 'rule' of not being able to say 'no', however fantastic the suggestion, appeals to students and they soon learn that fantasy, useless in itself, can lead to sense; they like the obvious appropriateness of technical vocabulary like 'hitch hiking', which depends on word association. The rules of the 'game' are quite simple:

- create a huge number of ideas collectively – quantity often leads to quality
- welcome wild, extravagant ideas – they may suggest something useful
- 'hitch hike' to combine and improve ideas – even small gains help
- banish all negative attitudes – negativism inhibits creation
- postpone critical discussion – later criticism can be deeper

Class 4b had reached the stage, as experienced brainstormers, when they were eager to provide their own officials – a secretary and a chairman. The secretary writes down the ideas on the board (preferably a double board) or on flip paper, and must be prepared to interpret handwriting in order to read back the list to the class on request. After an introduction by Miss and a reminder about the rules of brainstorming, the class chairman takes over. The chairman's duties are:

- to stop more than one person at a time from speaking
- to check negative attitudes, and to deal with evaluation and general discussion
- to make sure the secretary has time to get down all ideas on the board
- to make extra suggestions during gaps; in particular to direct the class towards unexplored ideas
- to keep the class working on the central problem, yet without restricting flights of fancy

- to call a halt to stage one – the generation of ideas – before moving on to the second stage of classifying and then evaluating ideas

Brainstorming in action

In 15 minutes 4b produced more than 60 ideas on accidents and safety, together with a fair amount of reasonable interchanges: the secretary could have done some grouping as he wrote on the board, but he started off writing on too grand a scale and had to fill in spaces at random. The class noted this error.

Ideas

doctors	home	work
men in raincoats	hospitals	old people
playing fields	falls	burns
babies	school	gas
government places	glue	fire
electric blankets	lead	TV
explosions	cuts	hockey pitch
nurses	ice	my old granny
motorbikes	floods	swimming pool
animals	signs	dangerous goods
collecting facts	second hand things	instructions
pythons	RoSPA	pedestrians
horses	snakes	newspaper articles
swing doors	prevention	wasps
Xmas tree lights	road signs	plastic bags
roads	planes	seat belts
police	laburnum seeds	glass doors
stairs	snow	cars
chip pans	poisons	electricity
medicines	first aid	not taking care
symbols	dogs	drugs
black mambas	weed killers	smoking in bed

Chairman and commentary

'Babies' ... 'motorcyclists' ... 'my old granny.'

'No, we can't have your old granny in. She's nothing to do with our work.'

'Yes we can, because she fell down the stairs an' broke 'er 'ip. Anyway, you can't say "no" in this game. It's in the rules.'

'Well, we'll put down "old people" then. And we'll have to write "stairs" as well – that's a cause. Stairs are dangerous.'

'I got two in one go!'

'Be quiet! What else is dangerous?'

'Wasps' nests' . . . 'snakes' . . . 'vipers, pythons, anacondas, mambas, black mambas, green mambas, yellow mambas . . . .'

'There aren't any yellow mambas. Anyway, that's enough snakes. They don't live here.'

'We're only hitch hiking. Aren't we, Miss? Anyway, you're saying "no" again and you can't.'

'Spiders, then. Tarantulas. *They* live here. One ran out of a bunch of bananas in my Dad's shop.'

Classification

The second stage – of classification, the deferred judgement stage – really needs to be dealt with while the sprawling writing is still on the board. Grouping similar words and ideas (and finding that sometimes one word fits into at least two groups), then ranking priorities for action and deciding how the material generated is to be used, gives the class the satisfaction of creating order out of very obvious chaos. Brighter students with strong self-motivation realise the possibilities of using brainstorming principles when they are working on their own, writing essays and answering exam questions as well as working on projects. They learn that the key question to keep on asking is 'and what else?' after each suggestion or solution; this little 'prompt' can keep the ideas rolling out. An additional self-motivating element is to number solutions, always writing down several more numbers in advance as a target to aim at.

Classification can be a solo, group or class activity. In this case it was a class activity; the secretary performed on the board with different coloured chalks as like was linked to like, after a preliminary discussion about possible headings and their order. *Types of accident* was their first heading under which they included falls, burns, cuts, poisons and explosions, ringing these all in red chalk, moving on to *who is most at risk*? with babies, old people, pedestrians and cyclists ringed in blue. Their third heading, *causes*, in green, was by far the biggest section with over 30 entries: they found the need here for subgroups, with animals being a generic heading that included dogs, horses, wasps' nests and snakes, and with the snakes forming yet another subgroup which they decided was not really necessary. Fourthly, they listed together, in yellow, *where are people most at risk*?; fifthly, in purple, *sources of help*; sixthly, in beige, *means of prevention*, which raised the question as to whether the Royal Society for the Prevention of Accidents might also come under other headings as well, such as *collecting facts* – their final heading, in white. They put off a decision as to whether collecting statistics should in fact come at the end, or whether it would be better at the beginning.

Who is going to do what?

It is now a case of matching groups to activities. How shall this be done: on the basis of an autocratic decision by the teacher, who will rely on known abilities and interactions? An alphabetic decision using class registers of boys and girls? By drawing group numbers out of a hat? If an essential part of project work is decision making, then here is an opportunity for action by students. It is essential to talk about group dynamics – yet another 'adult' word which can appeal to the status of a class – and about the possible composition or combination of each of the seven groups. Each group must contain people who can help to hold the group together, manage the group's affairs effectively, and carry out the particular task required. Every aspect of the project will need all available talent, energy and enthusiasm from each member. Tactful handling here makes certain that all the difficult, less desirable ('we don't want John – he smells'), and less able pupils don't find their way into one group. You can implement these rather difficult ideas by a kind of vote based on a standard list for recording individual preferences and by then putting these together in the form of a class matrix – yet another opportunity for a different skill to be learned and applied. This is a useful way of finding out what would command general support, and it helps the class to identify individual areas of common interest.

Individual preference chart

Name	Peter Tompkins
Rank	Aspect of project
7	Types of accident
3	Who is most at risk?
2	Causes
1	*Where are people most at risk?*
4	Sources of help
6	Means of prevention
5	Collecting facts

In the last resort, the conclusion on grouping has to be that it depends on your knowledge of the class, and that group structure will vary according to circumstance. The situation is more complex than in industry, where it is a question of matching personalities to activities so that the aims and objectives are fulfilled most effectively in the minimum amount of time. In

Class matrix — showing the popularity of causes and the unpopularity of data collection

Projects		Peter T	John S	Anita H	Dan L	Ahmed P	Sandra K	Kathy A	Sean B	Bob M	Louise S	Totals	Rank
1	Types of accident	7	3	4	3	3	4	3	3	3	4	37	3
2	Who is most at risk?	3	2	3	3	4	3	3	2	1	2	26	2
3	Causes	2	2	1	2	2	1	1	1	3	3	18	1
4	Where are people most at risk?	1	5	5	5	3	5	5	3	5	4	41	5
5	Sources of help	4	4	4	3	4	4	4	3	4	5	39	4
6	Means of prevention	6	6	5	5	7	6	6	6	6	6	59	6
7	Collecting facts	5	7	6	7	7	7	7	7	7	6	66	7

education, we have to consider in addition the long term needs of students as individuals and not be exclusively dominated by a neatly presented A4 folder for examination assessment. Who shall do what, and the processes by which this decision can be reached, are as important as the end result.

At the same time, in view of the difficulty in marking projects, you may decide that individuals have to work on their own, using their first or second choice from their individual preference chart. This means that several students are working on parallel subjects which will not necessarily produce an identical approach or an identical result. In the case of 4b, there was a known – and favourable – response to working in groups who already had an awareness of some of the pitfalls – 'no Sandra, you took the notes down last time, it's somebody else's turn now' – and a forthright realisation that it is very easy to perpetuate specialisations in doing the headings, the drawings, the photographs and the statistics. And though they accepted the need for a leader, they weren't going to be bossed around, and it wasn't going to be the same person every time. If a group does not become aware of these dangers itself through tactful guidance, you will have to supervise more stringently, to be on the look out for the development of an élite which suppresses the motivation of the others. In any class there will always be students who prefer to be on their own, to be different, to pursue an independent line of thought. In the case of 4b there were three reliable 'self-starters'. They all had the sense to confine their subject: electrical safety was reduced to finding out how many people could put on a plug properly, and how many appliances were sold with plugs already fixed – and if not, why not? The motorbike addict restricted himself to safety helmets: was present design safe, comfortable and attractive? How could misting up be improved? What did people use – raw potato, a slice of apple, soap liquid? What else could be done commercially? The quiz enthusiast set out to devise a CSE exam paper with true/false and multiple choice questions. She thought quizzes were a good way of learning things, and she wandered round the groups, a reporter pen round her neck, snapping up useful items. She decided to try out her quiz on her mother's Women's Institute, and see how they scored compared with a group of fifth formers.

What needs to be done?

It is a good idea to have some fairly specific ideas about the aim of the project as soon as a choice has been made and before the first enthusiasm has worn off. Group 1 can see quite clearly that they will have to collect reliable evidence in order to be able to find out the most common types of injury or death: 'It's only when we know what people die of most that anybody can think about stopping it.' Group 7 – the most reluctant group – realise that their task of collecting facts is very much the same as that of Group 1 and they decide to merge. There is some argument about who is going to be the chairman. Group 2 are aware that some sections of the community are more at risk than others. Which are they? They will function as a separate unit, but they will send a spy to see what groups 1 and 7 are doing. Group 3 need watching because their dominant personality is the snake enthusiast, who tries to direct the group into finding out how many dangerous reptiles are at large. He is in conflict with another member who feels strongly about child molesters ('men in dirty raincoats') after an incident involving his little sister. Nevertheless, order prevails, they develop a sense of proportion, and set out to obtain information from a variety of sources about the causes of accidents: if the causes are known perhaps people will stop selling, making and doing dangerous things. Group 4, working on places where people are most at risk, think they have a large subject to handle; they break up into subgroups dealing with home, school, work and leisure, and decide to find out the main hazards and how they can be reduced. They think they might get round to planning a campaign, perhaps concentrating on school to start with. Group 5 looks at the people and organisations who are involved in safety, either in preventing accidents from happening, or in helping people when one has happened. They decide to write a guide on 'what to do when an accident happens', with separate leaflets on different kinds of accidents. They might even make posters as well, and a tape recording. Group 6 think preventing accidents would save a lot of money (whose money, they want to know) and they will look at warnings, cautions, signs and symbols and test the understanding of various age groups. They might even find the need to suggest some improvements.

All groups, whatever their aim, are now aware that their project will fall into several stages:

- introduction – and statement of aim(s)
- collection and assembly of information and data
- period of investigation (questionnaire and survey, design)
- assessment and evaluation
- presentation and writing up (including contents, indexes, resources)
- conclusions and recommendations (with a brief summary)

They question whether their plan has to be done in exactly this order. Economically minded students feel that they could consider leaving the introduction (once they have orally clarified their aims) until the end and write up first and last together. They think that if they do the beginning at the end they may have a better chance of a good start, with a funny story, a dramatic incident or a good quote. They also decide that collecting facts could be going on at the same time as the first draft of a questionnaire. So a plan, they reckon, is just a sort of framework for guidance only, and you can move the bits around and put in extra items if these happen to crop up. And a plan points once again to the need to decide who is going to do what, and with whom.

When is it all going to happen?

Undoubtedly there will be the inevitable restrictions of a timetable, together with the problem that different groups or individuals will all be required to finish at the same time. Planning time is as important in skill learning as identifying aims: this can be done by means of a simple diagram called a Gantt chart. This chart enables you to illustrate the estimated time for any activity, using a bar or line, with a further line in a different colour or shade to show at a glance whether or not work is proceeding according to plan. Class 4b's 'safety' project was based on two periods a week for ten weeks. Take Peter's chart on electrical safety, for example. It was a rough and ready guide, but it did bring home to him the need to be realistic in estimating time, and to allow for contingencies. Quite rightly, he allowed only one block of two periods for going to the electricity showrooms because he asked permission to leave school in his lunch hour. However, he badly miscalculated over contact with manufacturers. His big mistake was in leaving his letters to companies until too late in his project: the letters themselves took a long time, there were more of them than he expected, and answers were slow to come back. Some never came at all.

Gantt chart for timing on electrical safety

Peter's chart (see below) is based on the following activities:

- obtain standard three pin plugs (not less than six), equivalent number of lengths of flex and screwdrivers, a stopwatch or watch with second hand
- draw up record charts with name, time taken to put on plug, correct or incorrect, if incorrect what was the mistake. Carry out classroom test
- write up classroom test
- prepare record cards for wider surveys *a* among staff and *b* at an old people's club. Carry out tests
- write up second tests
- Look at appliances in electricity showrooms, making a list of those with plugs already attached and those without attached plugs
- write letters to manufacturers supplying appliances without plugs
- evaluate and present results, making comparisons in age groups

Task \ Week	1	2	3	4	5	6	7	8	9	10
Obtain materials	▨									
Record cards and classroom tests		▨								
Writing up (1)			▨							
Other tests				▨	▨					
Writing up (2)						▨				
Looking at appliances							▨			
Writing to manufacturers								▨		
Presenting, evaluating results								▨	▨	▨

Where is the project going to be carried out?

More often than not, because of the short spans of time available, the main part of a project will be carried out within school or college. It is important to have a single room as a base, where you can display materials – where Peter can proudly put up his Gantt chart, where ever expanding folders can be stored for easy and quick retrieval from a good filing system. But even within the building itself there is a variety of free range activity that can take place. Peter, for example, intended to pursue members of staff at an appropriate moment to see how good they were at putting plugs on; the safety quiz was to be tested out on a different year group; group 4 would be prowling round school to find accident black spots. But there are times when investigations outside school are desirable – like working in this case with the Women's Institute or old people's club. It is then that certain precautions have to be taken. You must:

- obtain the consent in writing of each parent before a student leaves school during school hours. A simple form stating the purpose of the project, with space for a signature, is enough
- give each student who is in direct contact with the public (e.g. carrying out a survey or an interview) a card of authorisation signed by the head teacher or head of department: 'John Sutton is a pupil at Long Meadow School and is carrying out a social studies survey into the Saturday closure of banks. Signed: L. Farmer (head teacher).'
- advise the police if significant numbers of students are carrying out interviews
- ask and advise shops well in advance if you are planning any investigations
- check school insurance policies on liability for theft and injury during school hours
- arrange as high a ratio of staff to students as is possible
- organise a recognised assembly and departure point
- check up on basic equipment – pencils, hardboard for pressing on, questionnaires or record cards – before setting out, and look at what sort of shoes they are wearing
- hold a briefing session, stating clearly the point of the exercise, and outline acceptable behaviour in public
- hold a debriefing session immediately afterwards – even if it is in the car park or bus station – while enthusiasm and sense of achievement are still dominant

Preparing the tools for planning

Timetabling – making a 'guesstimate' as to how long a task is likely to take – is one of the planning tools that 4b's safety project has already thrown up. And in this case there are precedents – Gantt charts and critical path analysis – for guidance. Some students will never get the point or practice of either of these at all; some will be able to appreciate principles and develop basic strategies (realising that even simple operations like making a cup of tea produce complex diagrams); some will move on in later years to an appreciation of the critical importance of timing assessment in business and industry. But there are other planning tools which can help pupils to identify the complexities that lie between intention and achievement. Learning how to carry out an investigation or a survey, design a questionnaire and interview people are all techniques described in chapter 4, where there are again basic rules which can be learned and applied even at classroom level in the search for information. Here too an enormous variation in attainment is inevitable, and it may be that it becomes your job to design any necessary questionnaire, though there are still many colleges of education which fight shy of giving training in questionnaire design, in spite of its multidisciplinary uses, because it is so difficult to do properly.

But there are other planning tools which we ought to be able to expect most children to create for themselves: writing a job list, ranking the priorities, working out a simple order of events, making a list of equipment likely to be needed, with its possible cost and the places or people it can be obtained from. With less able children you can present a job list to be put in the right order, like this one on preparations for a foreign visit produced in a study of holidays:

- cancel milk and bread
- turn off gas, water and 'the electric'
- get ticket
- get passport
- leave key with neighbours
- go to the coin-op
- take aspidistra next door
- do shopping and get presents
- take cat to kennels
- get vaccinated
- cancel papers and *Woman's Own*

Which would they do first – turn off the gas or see about a ticket? The important, though indirect, message is that skills in the art of self-management matter more than those in getting a good mark for a particular project. The essence is in learning to think and to plan in an orderly and constructive manner, with tangible checklists (with the satisfaction of ticking off items in a well subdivided list) and records of what has been done and what still remains to be done.

Take Peter's electrical competence chart, for example. He borrowed the class list, having decided he was going to find out how good everyone was at putting on plugs. But he soon realised that he couldn't just have a column of names with ticks and crosses beside them, and that he would have to devise some sort of table as a planning tool:

Name	Sex?	Time taken	Correct	How many mistakes?	What sort of mistakes?
S Barlow	M	5 mins	yes	–	–
L Burroughs	F	7½ mins	no	1	brown and blue wires wrong way round

He was rather shocked at the size of his table – 'all I wanted to know, Miss, was whether they could or they couldn't' – but when he came to draft his form he realised that he was going to need much more detail for his investigation to have any value. He soon became aware in practice that 'sex?' was an unfortunate question, but he defended it on the grounds that L Burroughs was a Lesley and he never could remember whether that was male or female. He also appreciated that he wasn't going to have a happy time playing with the sports teacher's stopwatch if he had to do all the recordkeeping as well and watch out for the number and kinds of mistakes that people made. So he decided to ask for help, for a secondment from the combined groups 1 and 7.

Group 5 needed a different kind of planning tool in their look at the people and organisations who were involved in safety, either in preventing accidents or dealing with them when they happened. They organised a mini brainstorm within their group to produce more – and even personally named – examples of people they might need to be in touch with. Their first chart showed:

Name of student	Name of contact	Letter?	Visit?	Phone?	Reply
M Newbury	school nurse			✓	discussion group
P Jackson	DTI accident surveillance scheme		✓		list of statistics

But their second version added the dates when contact was made so that they could know whether they were likely to need to make follow-up calls and where the hold-ups were. Their final chart was the outcome of much discussion about who was to do what in the group, how individuals were to be contacted, and where names and addresses were to be found. It also included the date when a letter of thanks had to be sent.

Each of the groups needed some sort of a chart or record card at the planning stage, as well as in the future presentation stages dealt with in chapter 5. But such planning tools have to be custom made, according to subject, method of investigation, and ability of students. Your role here is very much one of an expert consultant, called in on demand, and letting controlled mistakes happen.

Finding out the facts

Finding and becoming familiar with relevant literature and resource materials has now become an important and time consuming part of education in general. Students' attitudes to collecting background information vary from misuse, which can sometimes be skilfully turned into corporate asset, to the achievement of considerable expertise. There are those who like to be left quietly alone 'to look up things in lots of different books and copy them down'; others, messily artistic, cut up magazines and glue bumpy extracts into their folders or flamboyantly adapt diagrams and charts with thick felt pens; others have jackdaw instincts in their indiscriminate collections of pictures, pamphlets and photographs; but others sift and sieve information available in their library or resource centre, producing a balanced, integrated and finally personalised report. But this last group unfortunately suffers in Britain from libraries that are often inadequate, out of date, short of the current periodicals essential for project work and deprived of their indexes. This problem is compounded by the fact that there can be considerable difficulty in finding resource materials at the right level of interest and understanding.

When British children first go to secondary school at eleven, they are taken on a trip round the library, told how to find books, how catalogues are arranged and what the rules are. But they are seldom taught how to compare and to question different sources of information, to know what to look for, to skim through to extract essentials, use indexes, hunt out, track down, record data systematically or make efficient notes. In other words they do not normally have the training in study skills on which the successful outcome of a project depends. The Schools Council's report in 1979, reinforcing the British National Libraries Survey, on *The Effective Use of Reading*, shows that secondary school children are 'rarely, if ever, taught the advanced reading skills needed for more academic study'. And study skills are an essential part of the research element of project work, whether relating to the traditional use of books and printed material or extending into the software of new technology.

Other sources of information

Since additional sources depend so much on the subject chosen, 4b's quest for background information on safety provides a specific example with underlying generalities. A brainstorm on possibilities produced a number of suggestions, some of which – like Acts of Parliament – they recognised as valid but remote: 'We don't reckon we'd understand much about them.'

1. They saw *themselves, their parents, teachers and acquaintances* as a potentially useful source of knowledge, a kind of human data bank, and the important thing was to know the right questions to ask in order to retrieve the information they wanted. They considered that what they knew – or could find out – from their own direct observation was as relevant as straight book knowledge.
2. The *community*, again people based, was seen as an essential resource for three main reasons: it's real, it's local and it's usually free. They could use the community in four main ways as a resource:

    - *people*, including staff, parents, the parent/teacher association, shopkeepers, policemen, traffic wardens, social workers, public or environmental health officers, nurses, ambulancemen, the school doctor, newspaper reporters, old people
    - *places*, including school itself, sports and leisure centres, football grounds, canals and rivers, accident black spots, advice centres, insurance offices, hospitals, clinics
    - *things*, including newspapers, directories (especially *Yellow Pages* if you knew your alphabet properly), local radio, hospital radio, council services
    - *needs*, including more pedestrian precincts, controlled crossings, schemes for young motorcyclists, fenced-off railway lines and canals, better accident and emergency cover at weekends

    Obviously, if the project had been on energy, pollution, town planning or money lending facilities, the detail would have been different, but the role of the community under these four main headings still remains valid.
3. Among *mass media communications*, television and radio

provided them with up-to-date and often spectacular information (though they couldn't always agree afterwards about what had been said, particularly about numbers); they thought that certain teenage and women's magazins, and technical journals, could provide ideas, information and stories about real people.

4 *Government departments* and public services, both local and central, could provide a free source of information. Local government departments, for example the Department of Environmental Health or the Road Safety Advisory Committee, would sometimes send a speaker round. Nationally, different ministries (and the Office of Fair Trading) would provide leaflets, fact sheets and posters, and loan slides, tapes and films. In 4b's case, they were dependent on statistics on accidents and emergencies produced by the home accident surveillance system and distributed, sometimes on a computer printout, by the Department of Trade and Industry. They also thought that certain HMSO publications might be difficult but useful.

5 *Acts of Parliament* and questions asked in the House of Commons and recorded in *Hansard*. In the safety project it was the Consumer Safety Act of 1978 which was the most relevant Act.

6 *Relevant organisations*, national and local, could be contacted on specific issues. In this case 4b approached RoSPA for magazines, newspapers, posters and leaflets, the British Standards Institution for information on safety standards for household products, the Health Education Council and the Health and Safety Executive. Locally, they found a list of organisations at the town hall and picked out the Electrical Association for Women and the St John's Ambulance Brigade.

7 *International organisations* and agencies, in this case the Commission of the European Economic Community in Brussels for details of directives on safety, and the International Organisation of Consumers' Unions in the Hague for information about its consumer Interpol – a worldwide warning system on dangerous products.

8 *Producers, manufacturers and their federations, and retailers*, in this case the British Gas Corporation and the Electricity Council as national examples, and the electricity showroom locally. Up-to-date trade directories are available in public libraries.

Assembly of facts   The algorithm on page 45, produced by the Centre for Consumer Education and Research in Scotland, shows how certain kinds of

Algorithm for fact assembly

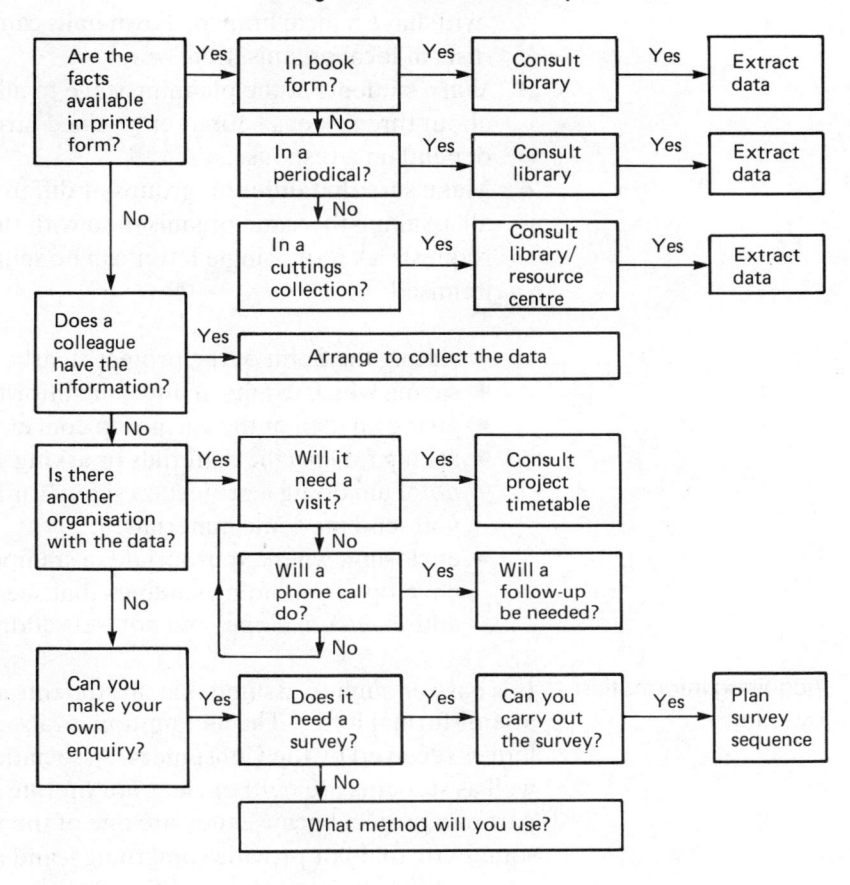

```
Are the facts available in printed form?
  → Yes → In book form?
            → Yes → Consult library → Yes → Extract data
            → No → In a periodical?
                     → Yes → Consult library → Yes → Extract data
                     → No → In a cuttings collection?
                              → Yes → Consult library/resource centre → Yes → Extract data
  → No → Does a colleague have the information?
           → Yes → Arrange to collect the data
           → No → Is there another organisation with the data?
                    → Yes → Will it need a visit?
                              → Yes → Consult project timetable
                              → No → Will a phone call do?
                                       → Yes → Will a follow-up be needed?
                                       → No →
                    → No → Can you make your own enquiry?
                             → Yes → Does it need a survey?
                                       → Yes → Can you carry out the survey?
                                                 → Yes → Plan survey sequence
                                       → No → What method will you use?
```

information and investigation lead on to the logical structuring of a project.

Problems in obtaining information

Students will be forced to communicate with some outside organisations in the course of their search for information. It can happen that an organisation with great goodwill and little money can receive a steady stream of letters from students in the same group asking for identical information. It is not unknown for a specimen letter to be put up on the board by a teacher and laboriously copied out thirty and more times by the class. Though communication skills are important, this is no part of the well run project. It is important to:

1 Check first in the school library or resource centre to see if the books, leaflets and materials your students may need are there. If not, try the public or county library service.

2 Find out if the organisations that they may need to be in touch with have a local branch. Town halls can help here; they have lists of local organisations.
3 Warn students at the planning stage to allow plenty of time – about three weeks – for a reply, since further action may depend on a response.
4 Make sure that different groups or different individuals are not all assailing the same organisation with the same simultaneous requests. A joint, single letter can be sent, with points clearly itemised:

- stating the point of the project clearly
- saying which exam – if any – the information is needed for
- giving an idea of the age group concerned
- asking for specific materials or asking specific questions – *not* 'I am doing a project on safety for my exam. Please will you send me some materials?'
- enclosing, where appropriate, a stamped addressed envelope (reminding students that sae means 'stamped addressed envelope' and not 'self-addressed envelope')

Acquiring information by letter

It is easy enough to assume that all students are capable of writing a semi-formal letter. The assumption is false: indeed some of the letters received by the Consumers' Association from teachers as well as students are neither clear nor literate. Letters appear as part of a project because they are one of the means of asking somebody to do or provide something – and a favourable response is more likely if the communication does not offend or irritate. The following checklist is intended as a guide:

1 Before beginning to write be sure that you know what you want to say and the order in which you want to say it.
2 Decide whether you are going to use official printed school notepaper, or whether you will have to write or type the school address at the right hand side:

Longmeadow School
Barnacres Lane
Fallowfield LT1 3TD
Wexfordshire

Put the date beneath: 11 July 1984.
3 Check up on the full name of any organisation you write to, and set it out at the left side of your page.

4   If you know the name of the person you are writing to, use it and spell it correctly; it is discourteous to address Mr Sharp without an e, if that is the way he spells his name. If you are writing to an organisation, find out the specific department you need and then address your letter 'Dear Sirs'.
5   Decide if you need a heading to appear underlined immediately underneath the person(s) you have addressed, eg <u>Project on dangerous toys and equipment.</u> This can help to shorten your letter, and also to enable it to reach the right person in an organisation sooner.
6   Make clear in your opening paragraph your reason for writing.
7   Be as brief as is consistent with covering all the necessary points.
8   Cover your subject in a logical order.
9   Start a separate paragraph for each subdivision of the subjects. (Letters do not normally have less than two paragraphs, even if the second is very short.)
10 Decide if you really do need a closing paragraph. If your letter has followed a logical sequence, it brings itself to a natural end and a final paragraph would be either an anticlimax or a meaningless and stereotyped formula. If an end is necessary, sum up the letter and point the way ahead.
11 If you start 'Dear Mr Sharpe', end 'Yours sincerely'; if you start 'Dear Sir(s)', end 'Yours faithfully' with your own name appearing legibly and in full.
12 Keep a carbon copy.

Example 1: a bad letter

>Longmeadow School
>Barnacres Road
>Fallowfield
>July 11

Dear Sir

I am doing some work on toys. Please send me some of your information.

Yours truly

A Cooke

47

Example 2: a good letter

> Longmeadow School
> Barnacres Road
> Fallowfield
> Wexfordshire LT1 3TD
>
> 11 July 1984
>
> The Education Officer
> British Standards Institution
> 2 Park Street
> London W1A 2BS
>
>
> Dear Sir
>
> <u>Project on dangerous toys and equipment</u>
>
> We are a fourth year group doing a project on toys and equipment that may be dangerous to babies and small children. This work is part of our CSE social studies course.
>
> Please send our group details of any relevant British Standards, and your booklet 'What every mum and dad should know', for which I enclose x pence in stamps.
>
> Yours faithfully
>
>
> Alan Cooke

Problems in assessing information

Whatever the source of the information – governmental, public, semi-public, private, commercial – there is always the possibility of some kind of biased representation. UNESCO's Director General, who has a keen interest in education, emphasised this strongly at the 1975 International Conference on Education in Geneva: 'Because of the considerable volume of information which the child like the adult receives, it is indispensable that the teacher should teach his pupils to sift and screen and classify this vast heterogeneous mass of facts, inaccurate interpretations and more or less tendentious messages.' So, having taught students to track down information, we now have to teach them to be sceptical about it, to refuse to accept things at their face value just because they appear in print or on the TV screen – to persuade them instead to cross check and compare, particularly interpretations of statistics. Bias is most likely to appear in commercially produced materials, where a lifetime's allegiance to a bank, building society or baked bean producer is at stake. It is worth noting that in the USA the Society of Consumer Affairs Professionals (SOCAP) has established a code of practice that distinguishes clearly betweeen promotional, information, and educational materials. For educational materials, the minimum standards are:

Accuracy   Statements are consistent with established fact or with prevailing expert opinion on the subject. Information is current, not only at the time the material is produced but throughout the time the sponsor distributes it.
Objectivity   All major or relevant points of view are fairly presented. If the subject is controversial, then arguments in favour are preferably balanced by arguments against; at the least, the sponsor bias is clearly stated, and references to opposing views are made.
Completeness   The materials contain all relevant information and do not deceive or mislead by omission.

These three points from the SOCAP code are worth remembering in places where, and at times when, the best produced materials are produced free for students and teachers by commercial concerns. The choice can be a bitter one – bias or nothing. The children of Kenya have excellent materials and first rate sources of information produced more or less solely by Brooke Bond. But are they aware that any other brand of tea exists? Nevertheless, the detection of bias, the evaluation of information for dispassion, is all part of the basic project exercise. To make students aware that there is a potential problem, you can get them to complete the form on page 50. Thinking about the issue may provoke solutions.

Storage and retrieval of project information

For most written projects – in commerce and business studies, social and environmental studies, home economics and history – the basic unit is likely to be an A4 looseleaf system, with pages kept in a coloured card folder which can also contain cuttings, pictures and photographs. Members of a project group ideally have the same coloured folder for quick identification, with peel-off sticky labels naming the individual and the aspect of the project the student is working on. Access to a filing cabinet for

Evaluating consumer information

Throughout your life, you are going to have to make sound decisions on what to 'buy' – both in terms of goods and services and in terms of ideas. Here are some questions you should ask yourself as you study consumer information before you make your 'buying' decision.

Product
Service
Issue _____

1 Who prepared this consumer information? _____
_____

2 Why did they produce it? _____
_____

3 Are they trying to convince me of something – what to buy or what to think? _____
_____

4 How complete, objective, and reliable is this information? _____
_____

5 Do I need to know more before I make a decision? _____
_____

6 If so, what do I need to know? _____
_____

7 Where can I find it? _____
_____

communal storage has two advantages. It minimises the risk of loss and prevents the dog eared battering of thin cardboard containers which will have to be presented for final assessment or even public display; it also provides the opportunity for appreciating the significance of, and therefore learning to operate, a proper filing system with appropriate cross referencing.

But, unfortunately, a 'projector' can't store everything because there simply isn't room; this means that data have to be collated and summarised, with references carefully noted in case a check has to be made in the final stages. It also means that there has to be a ruthless throwing out of items of doubtful value. A good projector also has to update his files from time to time (particularly in a longer term project) since figures rapidly become superseded. The merit of such a review is that it gives the chance to take stock of what is there, to reject items which are no longer relevant, and to revise.

The need to know Whatever the type of project, information properly assessed is the starting point: what has been done before, particularly if it is a question of a design project? Who has done it, and what were their problems and their conclusions? How has it been done? There is a great stock of information for any subject that is likely to come up within the school or college framework, and there are increasing possibilities opening up for computerised storage and retrieval. Such information, assembled wisely and with discrimination, and scrutinised for gaps, leads on to the next step – of tapping in personal knowledge and experience, of adding local information based on purpose designed inquiries and investigations. In their turn these too add to the existing supply of information about what people need or want and how they behave and respond. Since President Kennedy's address to Congress in 1962 there has been an increasing emphasis on the right to information. In the context of education, the stress is on recognition of the need to know.

4 Skills and strategies

No two projects are ever the same in method, intent or outcome: each has the stamp of personality, whether group or individual, impressed upon it. For choice is of fundamental importance in project based learning, not only of subject as far as is possible within the constraints outlined in chapter 2, but also – again within certain parameters – in the method of approach. Inevitably, there is some overlap between the planning tools described in chapter 3 and the strategies to be developed in this chapter; and just as there were general rules to be learnt about planning for particular circumstances, so there will now be a hard core of guidelines to be adapted at will in the implementation and development of techniques.

Background information, also an integral part of the preparatory stage, points the way forward in provoking new questions to be asked and answered, in raising problems to be solved, in stimulating ideas, suggesting possibilities for action and revealing gaps in knowledge. We are now approaching the most potentially independent part of a project: 'It's when we find things out for ourselves.' This is at the heart of discovery learning, leading to self-satisfaction and self-fulfilment as well as contributing to existing knowledge, or even bringing about improvements of practical benefit to others. The emphasis is on activity – on the discipline of evaluated activity – and on the belief that even young students can have the power to initiate change, sometimes simple but always meaningful and memorable. A study of school sports facilities showed that the showers had slippery floors, that half doors to lavatories were unpopular, that locks were rusty or totally removed. The result? Grateful comments and immediate alterations.

No single project will incorporate all the strategies suggested in this chapter, and keen students will have different experimental ideas of their own. The examples given provide the opportunity to choose and adapt according to circumstance – whether of ability, opportunity or even finance. In some cases it may be that some of the investigative skills needed to carry out a survey are almost as unfamiliar to the teacher as to the student.

Carrying out a survey

The point of a survey is the systematic collection of information you can't get by any other means – whether factual data or details about what people think – using a selected sample of the population. Manufacturers, for example, need to find out at an early stage whether a new product will sell, how much people are prepared to pay and who is going to buy it. The whole of the do-it-yourself industry, for example, is going to be affected by the results of its survey carried out in 1983 that it is women who are now the key decision makers in almost every area of the home improvement market. But manufacturers and retailers are not the only ones who need to base decisions on correct information. Government departments initiate social and economic surveys, like the Ministry of Agriculture, Fisheries, and Food's investigation into food consumption (national food survey, 26 June 1983): 'The average Briton is spending more money on food than a year ago even allowing for a rise in food prices.' Newspapers and television programmes commission market researchers to carry out national opinion polls on political attitudes, where questions are slipped in (in a 'blanket' questionnaire) amid information gathering on spreadable margarines, home insulation or pet foods. Once your students have grasped the basic principles, they can get a lot out of survey work, carrying over the skills they have learned into a range of additional subjects. They begin to think more analytically; they use English more clearly to avoid ambiguity, so that they don't get into Peter's situation when he wrote 'sex?' on his record card (as indeed many professionals before him have written 'born?', inviting the answer 'yes'); they learn the importance of sampling and simple statistical analysis; they communicate better in words and in writing; they work as a team; they recognise the importance of accurate recording and of checking findings at every step. This is hard discipline, but a context of reality provides strong motivation.

The three main types of survey

Observation

In *observation* surveys a questionnaire or even a simple form is completed by noting observations. This is the simplest type of survey to carry out from a classroom. Students can monitor world fluctuations in the price of copper or cocoa by checking commodity rates in the newspapers and by regular price sampling in shops; they can study foreign exchange rates in relation to sterling or the dollar – and find out what variation and commission apply to tourist rates; they can do a traffic count to find out, for example, how many mothers are still holding babies in their laps in the front passenger seats of cars; or they can study the accuracy of bus timetables and the facilities provided by public transport.

Respondent questionnaire

In the second type of survey, questionnaires are sent out for *completion by a respondent.* Organisations can afford postal deliveries and freepost envelopes for the return of questionnaires, but schools, colleges and charities have to rely on door-to-door distribution, or even distribution in the street. The former requires a return visit for collection, which may not be a bad thing if part of the project is getting to know the community better, whereas the latter requires a short questionnaire which people can fill in and hand back on the spot. Most *Which?* surveys are carried out this way: for example, what *The Sun* newspaper headlined 'Wear a skirt . . . and go up in the world', was a popular interpretation of the Consumers' Association's investigation into clothes to wear at work (March 1980) in which more than 1000 members' opinions were sought by post, topped up by an in-the-street survey in London. The majority of surveys carried out by *Which?* are much more serious, like 'What you think of your GP' (June 1983) where again members – 1300 of them this time – were questioned by post about waiting, getting an appointment, problems with receptionists, confidence in the doctor, home visits and so on. The response rate from members of an organisation is normally higher than that of the general public, so measures have to be taken to check that the sample is representative. Both of these examples are *opinion* surveys – what people think about a particular *issue* like electoral reform, the death penalty or the abolition of the House of Lords, where there could be controversy. But *Which?* also relies heavily on questionnaires to get information from people who *use* products: it can test only so many microwave ovens, typewriters, home computers or even cars, and consequently depends on the information provided by thousands of people who have had fairly long term experience of appliances or machines in their homes. In school you can ask what people think about corporal punishment, single sex schools or a voucher system for education: these would be opinion surveys, which you could carry out by means of a questionnaire to be completed by the respondent himself. Or you can set out to obtain factual information (in so far as people are honest and have reliable memories) by circulating questionnaires to find out about bicycles, binoculars or blow lamps: when did they last buy one? Was it from a specialist shop, a department store or through mail order? How much did they pay for it? How did they pay for it? Were there any defects on delivery? Were there problems over maintenance and repairs?

Interview

Thirdly, questionnaires can be *completed by the interviewer* who goes round school, work or the marketplace, or who knocks on predetermined doors, armed with his clipboard and ballpoint pen,

and his list of 'prompt' questions in case his respondent is reluctant to answer or doesn't seem to understand. People can also be questioned over the telephone, but this method leaves out 20% of the British adult population. These results are immediately available, always supposing that the interviewer is able to write quickly enough to get down all the information. Since students are often nervous about facing complete strangers, such surveys are best tried out in school or college first until interviewers become practised and able to cope with rebuffs. Was the cycle shed going to be big enough to cope with additional bicycles when bus prices went up yet again? How many people would want to use a cafeteria lunch system? How many would use a pay telephone in the entrance hall, and what sorts of problems (like vandalism) would have to be overcome? These are three practical examples chosen by student interviewers in a relatively small team carrying out a real survey. At the other extreme, students at the Collège Hohberg in Strasbourg interviewed 700 Alsatian farmers to find out about changing patterns of life. 'What do you think is the main crop in Alsace now?' they asked, 'Wine, wheat, cabbage? No – tobacco!'

The language they use

The jargon of market research has to be learned and understood, but even with less able students the fact that this is the language of real people doing real jobs provides a strong motivation.

Respondent This is the person selected by one of a variety of methods to answer the questionnaire or be interviewed by the interviewer.

Sample This is the number of people you decide to question. Time, money, energy, the degree of accuracy you are aiming at in your survey, all contribute to the number of people you ask. It is important to make sure that your *sample* is representative of your *population* – which may consist of people living in a particular town, students going to a particular college, local inhabitants using a particular leisure centre, or families who consume fizzy drinks. The main principle behind *sampling* correctly is that as far as possible you must avoid bias. For example, if your *population* is 200 men and 400 women and you select a *sample* of 10 men and 50 women, your *sample* will be biased in favour of women. Likewise, the place where you ask questions could cause bias, for example, interviewing people about the quality of school meals actually in the school canteen.

Simple random sampling This is not often used professionally but it can be used for speed and simplicity in school or college by picking out of a hat the first 50 names of the year group you are interested in.

Systematic random sampling Each person in the population has an equal chance of being chosen. If you have a list of all the people in your *population*, you can divide the total by your desired *sample* size to give you a sampling interval of 10, for example. Then you take every tenth person on the list and ask them your questions. But the interval may turn out to be much bigger. A fourth year social studies group investigating the shopping facilities that customers wanted in supermarkets used the electoral roll for the central wards of their town. They counted up the voters and worked out that they would need a sampling interval of 86 if they wanted a sample total of 400. What would they do if number 86 was not at home when they called? They decided that if a second visit was not successful they would try the next name on their list. But if the electoral roll or school register is not being used, it is important to make sure by other means that you cover all different types of people adequately. If, for example, you are involved in a survey of airport facilities, it is essential to make sure that you interview travellers at different times of the day and week so that you cover rush hour and off peak passengers whether businessmen, tourists, or school parties.

Quota sampling   'It's like when you get picked on by somebody standing outside the Odeon and asked to say what you think about some new sardine flavoured crisps.' The idea behind this specific definition is correct. Interviewers are told in advance that they must interview so many young people between the ages of 12 and 18. Quota sampling is done when you already know the proportions of different types of people in your population, and you select people according to these proportions. It is not done on the basis of 'friendly faces'!

Tally sheet   This is the record of your final totals. Unless you have sophisticated mechanical assistance – and a Scottish school stated quite firmly that 'in any future survey computer cards would be used for the answers to our questionnaires' – you will need some sort of tally sheet when it comes to sorting out your answers. This allows you to register how many of each possible answer you got – detailed working out of numbers is often recorded in the form of what are known as five barred gates, a device to make calculation at a glance easier in the counting stage:

Yes   ⵜⵜⵜⵜ ||| (= 8 replies)

No   ⵜⵜⵜⵜ   ⵜⵜⵜⵜ   ⵜⵜⵜⵜ ||| (= 18 replies)

You can tally all the questionnaires together, which will give the overall results of the survey. But if you want to look at particular groups of people in your sample separately – perhaps boys and girls or different age groups – you must first sort your questionnaires into these groups and tally the answers given by each group separately. The record survey later on in this chapter includes a sample tally sheet (see pages 67–69).

A survey presupposes that you are going to ask some sort of question, more often than not a whole series of questions; in other words, you will use a questionnaire. At its very simplest a survey can be a brief, fact finding mission with a straight 'yes' or 'no' or figures in answer to questions like 'How many pupils have access to a home computer or a calculator?' The findings can be represented by the simplest of bar graphs on outsize squared paper to suit the least able participant. However, there is no real point, and therefore no interest, until you start asking what sort of a computer or calculator is available, how much it costs, what it is used for and how often, and how good the instructions are. Only then, when this information is available, is it possible to start producing meaningful conclusions and even suggestions for improvements – in the presentation of manuals, for example. Such surveys within school or college have to be tactfully planned, however, so that personal possessions are not overvalued. It is not unknown for primary school topics to end in tears when young children learning to do graphs are asked what sort of car, television set, washing machine or video recorder their parents own.

Designing a questionnaire – asking the right questions

You can't ask the right questions until you are quite clear in your own mind what are the important aspects of the subject you are investigating. The Consumers' Association often has preliminary discussions with very mixed groups from different backgrounds, held under relaxing circumstances and surroundings, and led by an experienced interviewer who can draw people out. The major points, whether on mail order shopping, maintenance contracts, metrication or milk supplies, are then isolated and more often than not incorporated into a draft questionnaire. Even within the school context a group of class discussion, rather like the brainstorms already described in chapter 3, can highlight areas of particular interest – even if these have to be reduced to two or three simple questions which it is within the capability of your class to handle.

It can also indicate the structure of the survey (see the diagram on page 59). There is a tendency, particularly with keen bright students, to produce many logically grouped questions which are in themselves good questions but turn out to be daunting when they have to be analysed. Even if the creator of the questionnaire turns out to be the teacher, a preliminary discussion is again sound guidance on crucial issues, and will reveal the length appropriate for the class to deal with.

Here are two questionnaires on school meals. The first is very bad, but is not seen to be bad until the questions are tested on people in a pilot or *trial* run, tried out for ease of analysis, and assessed for the amount of useful information they provide.

Structure of a survey

```
            choice of
             subject
                │
                ▼
       ┌─────────────────┐
       │ what do you want │
       │    to find out?  │
       └─────────────────┘
                │
                ▼
┌──────────┐  ┌─────────────────┐  ┌──────────┐
│discussion│→ │     design of    │← │ research │
│  group   │  │   questionnaire  │  │          │
└──────────┘  └─────────────────┘  └──────────┘
                       │
                       ▼
┌──────────┐  ┌─────────────────┐  ┌──────────┐
│pilot test│→ │ implementation   │← │decision  │
│          │  │ and development  │  │on sampling│
└──────────┘  └─────────────────┘  └──────────┘
                       │
                       ▼
              ┌─────────────────┐  ┌──────────┐
              │collecting the   │← │preparing │
              │     facts       │  │a tally   │
              │                 │  │ sheet    │
              └─────────────────┘  └──────────┘
                       │
                       ▼
              ┌─────────────────┐
              │ analysing the   │
              │    results      │
              └─────────────────┘
                       │
                       ▼
              ┌─────────────────┐
              │    writing up   │
              └─────────────────┘
```

Example 1: questionnaire first version

A very bad questionnaire on school dinners

Q1 Which class are you in?
Q2 Are you male or female?
Q3 Do you have school dinners?   Yes/no
Q4 What do you think of school dinners?   Good/bad
Q5 How often do you have school dinners?
Q6 If you don't have school dinners, what do you do at dinner time?

Thank you for helping

Example 2: questionnaire final version and its tally sheet

School dinners questionnaire

Questionnaire no   Interviewer

Ask respondent

Q1 Which class are you in?   First year   ☐
                                        Second year   ☐
                                        Third year   ☐
                                        Fourth year   ☐
                                        Fifth year   ☐
                                        Sixth year   ☐

Q2 Sex of respondent   Male   ☐
                                        Female   ☐

Q3 How often do you have school dinners?   Every day   ☐
                                             Most days   ☐
If answer is 'every day' go straight   2 or 3 days per week ☐
to question 5   Not often   ☐
                                             Never   ☐

Q4 When you don't have a school dinner,   Go home to dinner   ☐
    what do you do instead?   Buy dinner elsewhere   ☐
                                            Bring food from home   ☐
                                            Have no dinner   ☐
                                            Other (please write in)

Q5 Do you think that school dinners are: Very good   ☐
                                             Quite good   ☐
                                             Neither good nor bad ☐
                                             Quite bad   ☐
                                             Awful   ☐

Thank respondent for helping

School dinners survey: tally sheet

Name of school
No in total group   No in sample

	Total	
	No	%
Question 1		
first year		
second year		
third year		
fourth year		
fifth year		
sixth year		
not recorded		

	Total	
Tally sheet cont	No	%
Question 2		
male		
female		
not recorded		
Question 3		
every day		
most days		
2 or 3 days per week		
not often		
never		
Question 4		
go home to dinner		
buy dinner elsewhere		
bring food from home		
have no dinner		
other		
Question 5		
very good		
quite good		
neither good nor bad		
quite bad		
awful		
Totals		

Points to note

1 The first questionnaire sheet has no number. A numbering system is essential so that you can check final totals and spot any losses.

2 It also has no space for the interviewer's name. Again it is important to know who was responsible for completing the questionnaire on behalf of the respondent, even if it is only a case of not being able to decipher illegible handwriting at a later stage.

3 Q1 'Which class are you in?' appears in both questionnaires, but is extensively amplified in the second. The first one might produce answers such as 'Mrs Anderson's class', '3c', 'social studies' or 'commerce', depending when and by whom the questions were asked. The important thing in this questionnaire is to have an idea of the age range; hence the questions relating to year group. The tabular presentation in the revised questionnaire enables the interviewer to tick the appropriate space, and the analyst to add up the ticks.

4   Q2 'Are you male or female?' may at worst invite peculiar answers and at best require a full word to be written. The revised form is easy to record and collate.
5   Q3 'Do you have school dinners?' provides only for an all-or-nothing answer and is not likely to produce useful information. The new version, again in tabular form, opens up a number of possibilities, and in revised Q4 it probes further into the reasons why some people don't have dinners on some – or on all – occasions. Q3 now becomes unnecessary.
6   Q4 'What do you think of school dinners?' offers two possible answers – good or bad – whereas the new question gives a range of five possibilities, again to be filled in by ticks.

The reorganised questionnaire now looks longer, but it requires much less writing on the part of the interviewer since all questions can now be answered by a tick. And, most important of all, you will have obtained far more meaningful information in a form that is easy to collate using a tally sheet and convert into appropriate bar graphs.

Questions under consideration: a checklist

The good and bad questionnaires, which were actually produced by teachers at an in-service training course, show some of the problems – and their solutions – but there are other generalisations which must always be borne in mind:

1   Interviewers must be able to explain clearly, confidently and briefly the point of the survey to those they are questioning. Students need intensive training and practice sessions before they start interviewing the general public. If they are recording information themselves they must have the necessary skills and the appropriate materials (see chapter 3).
2   Whether the questionnaire is being filled in by the respondent or whether it is intended for self-completion, instructions, 'prompts' and questions must be clearly separated. Definitions must also be beyond dispute. What, for example, is a split level cooker? Some respondents might think it was one with an eye level grill. If you intend to ask questions about power tools and say at an early stage 'have you got a jigsaw?', the word 'jigsaw' is still ambiguous. It could even be said that the word 'dinner' was not properly defined – is it the traditional two course school canteen meal (which the teachers had in mind) or does it include the new cafeteria meals? Is it the same as 'lunch'?
3   Before ever you duplicate a questionnaire in large quantities for public distribution, do a pilot test; in other words, try out

the questions first on a group or class to see if they actually work in practice and if the answers can be analysed, bearing in mind the constraints of timetables. Make any appropriate alterations – such as adding 'can't remember' to a list of days of the week on which people wash their hair or go to a leisure centre.

4   Order and design must be logical, with the interviewer leading the respondent through, or the respondent completing his own form. Bear in mind that every time someone has to move his eyes to another part of the page, turn back, or turn over, the mistake rate goes up.

5   Order of questions must also be chronological: 'Why did you decide to buy a cassette recorder? How did you find out about the product? Where did you buy it from?'

6   Try to start with something interesting.

7   Most school questionnaires are likely to be typed and duplicated and therefore depend on the size print of the typewriter available. If, however, print is available, then it should not be below 10 point. Leave plenty of space on the sheet – a cramped layout does not encourage a good response – and plenty of room for written answers, particularly if elderly people are being asked to take part. Keep the gap between the question and the place for its answer as small as possible.

8   Devise questions with recording and analysis in mind – laying out questions in the simplest way involves the least time for people filling them in and for those collating results. Commercial questionnaires now have computerised coding to deal with their large numbers of respondents. Students doing computer studies may want to work out a coding system, but for relatively small school surveys clear numbering and labelling of subquestions is still adequate – and has the advantage that it is very easy to split up questions for different students to analyse.

9   Leave any sensitive areas until the end – for example, questions about age. The traditional grouping for age looks like this:

18–24
25–34
35–44
45–64
65 and over

Having filled in the rest of the questionnaire, people will not want to waste their effort by not answering! And handle generally delicate subjects with care: instead of asking 'How often do you have a bath?', lead in gently. 'Some people find it difficult to take baths very often, what about you? How often do you have a bath? When did you last have a bath?'

10 Use short, simple words that everyone can understand, avoiding official, legal, technical, pompous language which bewilders people. 'Where is my *residence*, Miss?'

11 Write short, clearly worded questions. One school was goaded into devising its own questionnaire on six day trading because they found a copy of the question sent out to local shopkeepers: 'Are you in favour of the borough council making an order to exclude all shops in the High Street area of the borough from the provision of the Shops Act 1950 which requires shops (unless excluded by other provisions) to be closed for the serving of customers not later than one o'clock in the afternoon on one day in every week?' They knew this broke the rules. Could they do any better? They could and did.

12 Avoid condensed or elliptical English such as: 'if often, how often?', 'if other, specify here'.

13 Avoid leading questions, those using emotive words, such as 'Do you think we should give in to the communists?' and 'Do you buy cheap clothes?' which would not necessarily elicit truthful information.

14 Don't ask two questions in one, such as 'Do you suffer from sickness and headaches?', and avoid both hypothetical questions and those containing a double negative, such as 'Would you rather not use nonmedicated shampoos?'

15 Remember that precoded questions, with a list of answers for your respondent to choose from, are easier for you to analyse than open ended questions. Open ended questions expect the respondent to think up the answer on his own. The disadvantage of precoded questions is that you may put ideas into someone's head by providing a list of answers which should include 'Anything else?', and so bias your results. The disadvantage of open ended questions is in the analysis, which can be very laborious: you must first write down all the answers you got to a particular question, then group these together into categories that you think mean the same. Finally you make up a tally sheet designed to take these groups into account. As a short cut in using open ended questions in interviewing, you can use a continuum diagram with good and bad at the extremes, recording your interpretation of the reaction with a tick.

Good ☐☐☐☐☐ Bad

The results of asking open ended questions can be fascinating, and it is here that you get amusing and apposite comments to quote at the beginning or end of a report. In a Malaysian survey on television violence carried out by the Consumers' Association of Penang in 1983, children were asked what they would do to a criminal. Out of 50, 12 said they would 'shoot him dead'. Most of the others would box him, beat him, wall him up, poke him with a knife, hit him with a bottle, hang him or put him in a cage. Material suitable for a vigorous beginning to a project!

16 Point out what 'anonymous' means, and if names are mentioned, respect confidentiality.

Putting it all into practice: a survey on records and cassettes

This survey was first worked out for use in British schools by the Consumers' Association, with notes for students and separate notes for teachers for whom this kind of work might be new. It included a questionnaire and a tally sheet, which were then adapted for New Zealand students by the Consumers' Institute.

Buying records and cassettes

Questionnaire no ☐

Ask respondent

Q1 Are you:
under 14 years old ☐
14 years old ☐
15 years old ☐
16 years old ☐
over 16 years old ☐

Q2 Do you own any records or pre-recorded cassettes?
yes – records ☐
yes – cassettes ☐
no – none of these ☐

If none, thank respondent and end interview

Q3 Have you bought any records or prerecorded cassettes for yourself in the last 12 months?

Sex of respondent: male ☐
female ☐

yes ☐
no ☐

If no, thank respondent and end interview

Q4 If *yes*, which of the following sorts of records or prerecorded cassettes have you bought?
folk music ☐
jazz ☐
rhythm & blues ☐
top twenty music ☐
reggae music ☐
rock music ☐
progressive music ☐
soul music ☐
classical music ☐
spoken word ☐
disco music ☐
other – *write in* ☐

Q5 How many of the following have you bought for yourself, including with record tokens, in the last 12 months?

    singles
    LPs
    cassettes

Q6 At which shop or record club did you buy most of these records or cassettes?

Write in
    records

_____

    cassettes

_____

Q7 Why did you buy most of your records or cassettes from that shop?
Tick all answers agreed to

    cheapest ☐
    can listen before buying ☐
    have new releases first ☐
    near school ☐
    near home ☐
    buy other things from there ☐
    good selection ☐
    parents buy from there ☐
    staff there to advise ☐
    staff don't hate teenagers ☐
    will take records back ☐
    will take record tokens ☐
    other reason – *write in*

Q8 If you have bought both records and cassettes, why have you bought both? *Write in*

Q9 If you had the choice of the same recording on record or cassette, which would you buy:

    Record ☐
    Cassette ☐

Q10 Why would you choose that?
Write in

Q11 How much did you spend in the last 12 months on records and/or casettes?

    Less than $10 ☐
    $10 but less than $20 ☐
    $20 but less than $30 ☐
    $30 but less than $40 ☐
    $40 but less than $50 ☐
    $50 or more – *write in how much* $ ____

Q12 Have you ever bought records or cassettes which had something wrong with them?

    Yes ☐
    No ☐
If no, go to **Q18**

Q13 If *yes*, what was wrong with the record/cassette? (Answer for the last faulty record/cassette bought, if more than one)

Write in

Q14 Did you take it back to the place where you bought it?

    Yes ☐
    No ☐
If yes, go to **Q16**

Q15 If *no*, why didn't you take it back?

Write in

Q16 If *yes* at Q14, what happened when you took it back?

Write in

Q17 What did you feel about this?

Write in

Q18 Which of these do you have the use of at home?

Tick all answers agreed to
- Portable record player ☐
- Non-portable record player ☐
- Portable cassette recorder ☐
- Non-portable cassette recorder ☐
- Radio cassette ☐
- None of these ☐

If one or none of these, thank respondent and end interview

Q19 *If respondent has use of more than one of the above*, which of them do you use most often?
- Portable record player ☐
- Non-portable record player ☐
- Portable cassette recorder ☐
- Non-portable cassette recorder ☐
- Radio cassette ☐

Q20 Why do you use that one most often?

Write in

Thank respondent for helping, and end interview

Sample tally sheet
(Remember to leave plenty of room, especially for the open ended questions)

Name of school _____   No in total group _____

Address _____   No in sample _____

_____

	Total
Male	
Female	
Question 1 Under 14 years	
14 years	
15 years	
16 years	
over 16 years	

	Total
Question 2 yes – records	
yes – cassettes	
no – none of these	
Question 3 yes	
no	

	Total
Question 4	
folk music	
jazz	
rhythm & blues	
top twenty music	
reggae music	
rock music	
progressive music	
soul music	
classical music	
spoken word	
disco	
other	
Question 5	
singles	
less than 5	
5 but less than 10	
10 or more	
LPs	
less than 5	
5 but less than 10	
10 or more	
cassettes	
less than 5	
5 but less than 10	
10 or more	

	Total
Question 6	
records	
cassettes	
Question 7	
cheapest	
can listen to records before buying	
have new releases first	
near school	
near home	
buy other things from there	
good selection	
parents buy from there	
staff there to advise	
staff don't hate teenagers	
will take records back	

	Total
will take record tokens	
other	
Question 8	
Question 9	
record	
casette	
Question 10	
reasons for records	
reasons for cassettes	
Question 11	
less than $10	
$10–$20	
$20–$30	
$30–$40	
$40–$50	
$50 or more	
Question 12	
yes	
no	
Question 13	

	Total
Question 14	
yes	
no	
Question 15	
Question 16	
Question 17	
Question 18	
portable record player	
nonportable record player	
portable cassette recorder	
nonportable cassette recorder	
radio cassette	
none of these	
Question 19	
portable record player	
nonportable record player	
portable cassette recorder	
nonportable cassette recorder	
radio casette	
Question 20	
No of respondents who refused to help or could not be found _____	

69

This questionnaire on records was designed with young people's interests in mind to produce a potentially useful result. A readymade questionnaire like this is invaluable for teachers who are hesitant about their own or their pupils' purpose designed questionnaires, and yet who want to make a start on survey work. Local consumer groups in the United Kingdom frequently carry out investigations, and their national federation organises briefing packs of surveys with questionnaires, which could be used by schools, on grocery prices, banking facilities, public telephones and domestic services such as plumbing. They then put together the results of local inquiries to give a national picture. A second, more confident step is to take the results of a published survey, for example the fact that in 1983 58% of British people watch television in bed (or that 20% of girls wash their hair every day), and then work backwards to create questions. You can use *Which?* reports in this way, particularly because clear paragraph headings, whether on shoes, shirts, shampoos or student grants, give a strong hint of the questions that were asked in the first place.

Questionnaires in action

In many parts of the world the questionnaire – even if imposed by adults – is being used as an investigative teaching tool. Students find out in Malacca about teenage spending habits (Chinese children received more pocket money than Malay children in the same community); in Penang about public transport, refuse collection and recycling, hire purchase, food additives and pollution; in Korea about the price and availability of school books and stationery; in Karnataka about short weights and measures; in Maharashtra about food adulteration – is food a preserver or a destroyer?

The following two examples are the result of collaboration between staff and students:

Example: shop safety (Collège Hohberg, Strasbourg: translated from French into English

Shop safety

Name of shop [   ]   [M] [F]

1 Have you ever thought of the fire risk in this store?   [yes] [no]

2 Do you think there are adequate safety measures against fire hazards?   [yes] [no] [don't know]

3   Do you know what these measures are? | yes | | no |

4   Do you know where the fire exits are? | yes | | no |

5   Do you think you might panic if a fire broke out? | yes | | no |

6   In the event of a fire, would you be guided by the store's own personnel or would you decide what to do yourself?

| store personnel | | myself |

7   If a fire started here and now, how long do you think the fire brigade would take to arrive?

| less than 5 min | 5 min | 10 min | 20 min | 25 min | longer |

8   Do you think that the intervention by the fire brigade to prevent a disaster is | very quick | | quick enough | | too slow |

Asking and interviewing

Students tend to start off thinking that asking a few questions is easy enough after a short period of natural nervousness, and that all they have to do is to be able to get on with people: 'We were very worried at first about going up to people, even though we had practised muttering to each other: "I am a pupil from Buckdown School, and would like to know what you think about shopping in Withernsea. Would you mind answering a few quick questions?" Tina knew she would blush scarlet and she did. Shirley wondered what she would do if someone was rude to her. Lorraine thought she wouldn't be able to write down the answers fast enough. But after the first few times it got better, and Anne even began to enjoy herself. 'We didn't work on a quota sample basis; Miss says this means you ask a particular number of people between sixteen and twenty-four and others between twenty-five and thirty-four and so on. For one thing, we didn't want to ask people their ages, and for another we didn't think we'd be able to guess very well. But we did take care to get a collection of young people, of mums with babies and toddlers, of older women, pensioners and men – though two-thirds of the people we talked to were women. We included a blind man with a stick to see if he had special problems.'

Knowing the basic rules for introducing the survey, asking the questions, completing the answers and extracting personal details produces more accurate results – as well as building up self-confidence.

Introducing yourself

The interview you are carrying out may not be expected by the respondent (as in the case of this shopping survey) or you may have made an appointment. In either case it's important to make the right impression on people – which can mean checking up on appearances, perhaps by class consensus, in order to get the answers to questions.
Checklist for students

- introduce yourself by name
- say who you are doing the interview for
- state quite clearly what you are trying to find out
- produce evidence of who you are – a signed card or letter of authorisation from school
- emphasise that remarks are confidential (unless you intend to publish your results in a magazine or newspaper)
- tell the person you are interviewing how he was chosen

General comments

- keep your interview brief and to the point
- nevertheless, it is not impolite if you are standing in a cold wind on the doorstep to say, 'please may I come inside to ask my questions as I have rather a lot of papers'. It is as well for young, inexperienced interviewers to work in pairs: even so, two seventeen-year-old sixth formers were exposed to more information than they expected
- don't say that the interview will only take a few minutes when you know very well it will take at least half an hour; on the other hand don't stress the length of time too much
- if you are introducing your survey to someone who is not expecting you, you will have to be more careful about what you say than when you have made an appointment in advance
- vary the way in which you introduce the survey according to the type of person you are talking to: an elderly person who is suspicious – even frightened – and hard of hearing will need more reassurance and repetition than a young housewife

Asking the questions: advice to pass on to students

There are three main groups of questions: those designed to find out facts, those designed to find out what people think, and those designed to find out what people know. The answers to all three types of questions may be affected by the way you ask the questions: so the first rule on any question is to ask it exactly as it stands. Don't change the wording at all – if there are several of you doing the same interviews and you all change bits of the question you will probably end up by altering the meaning.

You may only get part of the answer you need, or the question may have been misunderstood; in this case, any further steps you take to get a more complete or more accurate answer are known as 'probing'. There are various ways of doing this, which depend on the type of question you are asking:

1. **Probing on factual questions** Don't ask leading questions that put ideas into people's heads either positively or negatively. Instead of saying 'you couldn't be more exact about the cost, could you?', be more straightforward: 'Could you tell me what the actual cost was, please?'. Use any kind of open question which does not suggest things, and do assist people in remembering when something happened. Ask when, where, how, what for and why – and use a calendar or diary to take people's minds back to the time when they last used registered post or bought a pair of winter boots. 'When did you last register a letter or parcel at the post office?' can be probed like this: 'Can you remember roughly when this was – did you do it before or after Christmas?' If the answer is 'before Christmas', then you have to think of another peg on which to hang your probe. 'Did you send any of your family a registered packet, perhaps for their birthday?' In the last resort do accept a 'don't know' (written down as dk) or 'don't remember' answer rather than force people to give you an answer just to please you. British interviewees are known to be eager to please!

2. **Probing on opinion and knowledge questions**
   - don't deviate *at all* from the wording of the question
   - repeat the question
   - look up expectantly, smile genuinely to give confidence, but don't overdo it
   - use phrases like 'could you explain a little more fully . . . what you mean by that?' or 'in what way?' or 'how?', repeating the relevant part of the question
   - don't suggest anything such as 'but what about so and so?' or 'oh, do you think that?' Don't overprobe, and remember that sometimes a person genuinely does not know
   - don't ask 'anything else?' or 'are there any other reasons?' until it is quite clear that there is no more to be said

3. **Probing in practice** Supposing that you want to find out people's opinions on traffic-free precincts, you could say: 'We sometimes hear that there should always be a shopping area in

a town which is free from motorised traffic. Do you agree with this idea?'
- yes   1
- no   2
- dk   3

If the answer is yes or no, you'll want to know more, so say 'why do you think that?' You may well get the lazy, uninformative answer, 'because it's better.' This is no practical help and doesn't tell you why, so your following conversation may sound something like this:

Probe	Answer
In what way?	Well, it's better for the children.
How is it better?	Well, it means that they can go to the shops by themselves. They don't have to bother about traffic and risk getting run over.
Anything else?	No fumes or noise from cars.
Anything else?	Nicer for everyone.
Could you explain that a little more?	It's safer for adults too, and you have more room to walk about and push a pram. You can sit down too and enjoy things.
Anything else?	No.

Prompting

This is a technique used in interviewing where it is necessary to suggest possible answers to a particular question and get people to choose one of the answers; this makes it easier for respondents, but you should introduce it with care. If they want to qualify an answer, or say, 'well, it all depends on . . .', then repeat the question together with the words 'in general', 'on the whole' or 'which comes nearest to your own opinion?' There are two ways of prompting – which once again you will have to practise within school before trying it out on the public. Firstly, a list of precoded items will have been provided as part of the question, and one way is to go straight through the list, reading all the answers out clearly and not pausing very much in between. Here is an example where an opinion question requires a generalised answer:

Would you say the problem of pollution today is:

	very serious?	1
running prompt	fairly serious?	2
	not at all serious?	3
do not prompt	don't know	

And here is an example of a factual question:

How long have you lived in this town (city, village)?

<table>
<tr><td rowspan="4">running prompt</td><td>5 years or less</td><td>1</td></tr>
<tr><td>5–15 years</td><td>2</td></tr>
<tr><td>15–30 years</td><td>3</td></tr>
<tr><td>over 30 years</td><td>4</td></tr>
</table>

Secondly, you can treat a list as an individual prompt because a reply is needed to each item as you go along. For example, in a survey on the shopping needs of old people – which many schools carry out – you may ask:

Do you usually have any difficulty in:

		yes	no	dk or na
	carrying a full shopping bag	1	2	7
individual prompt	getting small enough quantities of food such as butter, bacon ...	3	4	8
	getting anyone else to do the shopping when you are not well	5	6	9

Any question which needs prompting should be labelled clearly on the interviewer's form with the type – running or individual – required. In general, don't prompt 'don't knows'.

Sometimes you may want to print the form of words for the answers on a card, and hand it over to the person you are interviewing after you have explained the use of the card and read out the items. Watch out for any difficulties with poor sight or reading ability – people who say they haven't got their spectacles with them!

Recording your information: a checklist for students

It's no use practising your questions, asking them perfectly, making no suggestions and no assumptions, if you don't get down exactly what people say:

- always write the answer down at the time of the interview. Don't go off for a quick chat and think you will leave it until later
- deal with the code on your questionnaire accurately and systematically – this may mean ringing certain words, ticking or crossing out according to agreed practice
- cross out any question which does not apply to the person you are talking to

- write down the answers to any open opinion questions exactly as they are given. Don't give a précis of what they say or change the wording at all. Write in the first person and start writing as soon as they begin to reply
- make sure your writing is clear because someone else may have to analyse the results. If you think it will be helpful you can add your own comments
- check at the end of the interview that you have asked every question

Free interviewing

Sometimes you will not use a series of set questions; instead, you will be making up your own to gather facts and opinions from the person you are interviewing. The methods are very much the same, but you have to be more adept, more flexible and even more opportunist. Your own list of suggested questions may turn out to be useless, your own control of the situation more limited, if you are faced with an unstoppable flow of pent-up words and emotions. In these circumstances, the art of being a good interviewer lies in being a good listener, in finding an unexpected compatibility with the most unlikely people.

The following interviews are part of two projects, one on travellers and the other on old people. The first is from a tape/slide presentation produced by fifth year students working on a social education project, and the second is from a fourth year social studies investigation into the problems of the elderly.

Example 1: conversation with a traveller

Student:	Can you look into the future and things like that?
Traveller:	If I could, I wouldn't.
Student:	Wally said his parents could.
Traveller:	Well Wally can a little. I can have a dream and it would probably come true. I can dream of something to do with death and I always hear of somebody else.
Student:	Do you know of anyone that does it for a living?
Traveller:	Telling fortunes you mean? The old lady down the bottom.
Student:	Is she good?
Traveller:	Mrs Taylor? Yes, she can see into the future.
Student:	Does she have a crystal ball?
Traveller:	I don't know, she might do. Wally's mother used to years and years ago.
Student:	Do you ever go round selling pegs?
Traveller:	No, I used to. When I was single I used to. You

	walk your legs off that's all. There's no fun in it now calling door to door. Mind you I was only about ten then, I used to go alongside me Mum you know.
Student:	Have you ever set up stalls in a fair?
Traveller:	Me Mum used to, me Dad, but not me. I wouldn't jump into their shoes after they'd jumped out. I've had a pony and cart – brought up with a pony and cart – lorry, scrap iron, we used to do a lot of things. My husband, he used to do everything before I knew him, after he came out of the army. You name it he'd done it.
Student:	You say you were brought up being moved along, can you roughly say how many times you have been moved?
Traveller:	Thousands of times by the police. It's only this last four to five years that I've been settled on a site. They can't move us no more because they've got the district council now. Apart from that I have spent most of my life up and down the roads, moved all over the shop.
Student:	How do they make you move on?
Traveller:	If they come civil to us and ask us to move then we move, if they come and say, 'come on you've got to move out of it', a bit sharp, then we don't move.
Student:	Then they have to ask you politely?
Traveller:	When you get a pig to you that says 'you've got to go', and all this business, then it's bad.

Example 2: conversation with an old lady

Student:	What were things like when you were a girl?
Mrs Watson:	I didn't have no shoes when I was little. The streets they were all cobbled and they hurt my feet and I got chilblains something dreadful in winter.
Student:	Chilblains?
Mrs Watson:	Chilblains. On my hands and feet. I don't know whether they hurt or itched most. My mam used to put mustard on them or onion skins if we had an onion, but they still burst. I cried with the pain of them . . . . I didn't have any new clothes, neither, not of my very own, and when winter come my mam sewed my clothes on me so as they didn't come off till spring. The doctor come to the board school one day and he wanted to look at my chest I was that wheezy. But my mam say, 'you can't. I've

got 'er sewn up for t'winter.' And he didn't. He couldn't beat our mam. No one could.

Mrs Watson was over eighty, she thought, and was in an old people's home.

Opportunities for the less able

The laboriously slow writers, or even the nonwriters, can still get good results by unobtrusively using tape recorders and learning to edit. Knowing the stigma of failure in one medium they can start anew in a different medium, becoming experimental, incorporating old time music (among which they include the Beatles 'When I'm sixty-four') and producing a magazine programme on Christmas fifty years ago.

But whatever medium they choose, they have to accept that they are in control, albeit gently and unobtrusively: avoiding irrelevant digressions; keeping the pace moving or indeed sometimes slowing it down; seeking amplification of particular points of interest; interrupting if necessary to divert the flow with crisp but friendly interjection of a 'really!', 'yes', 'I see'; handling delicate issues carefully and never hinting at reproof or ridicule; being prepared to draw points together from time to time and round them off.

The following checklist can provide teachers with an unobtrusive guide to the assessment of students in action, or it can be used by students in appraising each other.

Checklist for interviewing

- Did the interviewer prepare the questions properly?
- What did the interviewer do to put the person being interviewed at ease?
- Did the interviewer prejudge the issue?
- Did the interviewer give the person being interviewed the chance to speak at length?
- Did the interviewer obtain enough relevant facts?
- Did the interviewer round the interview off properly, remembering to say thank you?

Testing and research

Chapter 3 dealt with the need for background information as a preliminary to any project. It pointed to ways in which resource materials reveal gaps in knowledge or emphasise the need for additional research about a special locality. Surveys and the questionnaires they often incorporate as an essential feature, are not however the only means of obtaining accurate, supplementary material. *Comparative testing* is a method which has become increasingly well known in industrialised societies in postwar years through the activities of consumer organisations.

Comparative testing: what is it?

'It's trying out bits of instant pud and Lyons Harvest Pies outside the Odeon.'

'It's a sort of market research to find out what people want.'

'It's finding out which of lots of similar things is the best.'

'It's comparing prices to see who is cheating.'

'It's a sort of government check to see if prices have gone up or down.'

These were the replies from a group of British sixteen-year-olds doing business studies, with the third answer being nearest to the true definition. Comparative testing, then, means carrying out the same tests on a number of similar things and seeing how they compare. Doing the *same* tests means that you have to make sure that the conditions of the tests are the same – the way the tests are done must be the same and the way the results are given must be the same. Good comparative testing is fair, accurate, objective, repeatable – and its results are of practical value.

It must be *fair*. If, for example, you are testing a number of things, like light bulbs or torch batteries, you must make sure they are all in the same condition when you test them. It would be no good comparing a new bulb or battery with one that had been kept a long time or was partly used. The circumstances too of the test must be the same. If you want to test fluids and correction papers for removing typing mistakes, your results will not be valid if you use different ribbons and grades of paper. Likewise, it is not fair to test something beyond its intended capacity or range. This means the things you are comparing must actually be comparable. Tests on a cheap portable record player will show that its sound quality is much worse than that of an expensive hifi set. You have to decide whether it is fair to compare the two.

Tests must be *accurate*, and checked at every stage. It is so easy to misread comments. Numbers also cause problems, especially if someone is in the habit of using a continental 1, which can be mistaken for a seven, or using a comma for a decimal point. Time can be an obstacle to accuracy, and students in their eagerness to finish may falsify results just as they could equally write up fictitious interview forms. The message has to go over that it is sound business practice for different individuals to carry out checks and if necessary rechecks.

Tests must be *objective* in that the views, opinions and prejudices of the testers must not be allowed to influence the

79

results. Tests must be designed so that opinion is eliminated: brand names should be hidden and alphabetical codes used wherever possible, people should not know the prices of the products they are testing, and they should not say what they think (or indeed listen to other opinions) about the brands they are testing. This is particularly difficult to avoid if your class is doing a comparative taste test on cola drinks, instant coffee or packet soups, where spontaneous and sometimes unprintable comments would be the normal reaction.

Tests must be *repeatable* if you are going to be able to use the results to make any kind of recommendation. If you can't repeat a test showing that something doesn't perform well, then there is little point in doing it in the first place, and it isn't fair to manufacturers. In the case of a professional consumer organisation, manufacturers would be quick to make accusations about printing misleading information if tests could not be repeated time after time, proving that something didn't work properly.

So who carries out comparative testing?

Manufacturers spend a lot of time and money on quality control to achieve consistency of output, to conform to standards, minimise consumer dissatisfaction and cut down on production costs. They usually just concern themselves with their own products. Consumer organisations in many countries – Australia, Germany, Hong Kong, Israel, the Netherlands, to name but a few in addition to the United States and the United Kingdom – also spend a lot of money on independent systematic comparisons of *a whole range* of products. They set out to reveal important interbrand and intermodel differences – the sort of thing that people can't usually find out for themselves by observation, reference to trade leaflets or their own five senses, about vacuum cleaners, for example.

Example: testing vacuum cleaners
Since vacuum cleaners are an essential household appliance, consumer organisations test them at frequent intervals. In its tests the British Consumers' Association uses two different kinds of carpet that ordinary families are likely to buy – a Wilton carpet which is fairly easy to clean, and a long pile nylon carpet which is very difficult to deal with. The first step is to make sure that the carpet samples are absolutely clean: this is done by a specially designed carpet beating machine. Then the carpets are made dirty again, this time with a known and controlled amount of standardised dust which is rolled in to get the effect of treading in dirt.

The vacuum cleaner, fitted with a new dustbag, is weighed. The balance has to be very accurate, for though the cleaner itself is heavy, the amounts of dust to be picked up from the different carpets are small. Tests are all carried out in a room where temperature and humidity are controlled – it's essential that all the cleaners should be tested under identical conditions. Testers clean the carpets at a set speed, keeping in time with an electric metronome and moving in a zigzag pattern, going over the carpet five times. Then the cleaner and the dust in its bag are weighed; by subtracting the weight of the empty cleaner and bag from this new reading, it is possible to find out how much dust has been picked up – and therefore how efficient the cleaner is.

Three different testers repeat these tests three times, and one of them tries out a second sample of the cleaner to make sure there was nothing unusual about the first. So, for each model, there are now 12 results for each type of carpet.

This is an example of a basic test. Others deal with electrical and mechanical safety, the ability of cleaners to remove dirt from cracks and crevices and from close up to skirting boards, and the variability of cleaners according to the fullness of the dustbag. All these tests, which are carried out under laboratory conditions, are supplemented by *user* tests: that is, by getting a panel of members to use two different cleaners a week in their own homes and fill in a questionnaire recording what they think are good and bad features.

What are the characteristics of a test?

Any product can be described only in terms of its characteristics. When you are comparing products, you have to decide which characteristics are relevant and which matter most: for example, a crash helmet must be safe, its chin strap must not slip and the casing must not crack on impact with the ground. It is a good idea to start off by listing all the characteristics of the product and then decide which are important to your class and which are within their capabilities to test. A basic list might look like this:

- Is it safe?
- Does it work well?
- Is it convenient to use?
- Does it last a reasonable length of time without going wrong?
- How much does it cost?
- Is it expensive to run?
- How attractive is it to look at?

Some of these questions involve a good deal of preparation – going and looking in shops, writing to manufacturers for specifications and to the British Standards Institution for information on standards and tests – before you can decide which activities are possible for you and your students. Obviously, tests for different characterstics will not be the same, and sometimes – particularly in a school – it will be impossible or too expensive to test some characteristics. The only way to deal with this sort of problem is to state quite honestly what has had to be left out.

Checklist for testing by students

- define the aim or purpose of the test
- list the characteristics of the product
- decide which characteristics are important, and define the scope of the project
- work out how long the test will take (do a Gantt chart or even critical path analysis)
- work out how much it is likely to cost
- if it is going to take too long or cost too much, then redefine and simplify the test
- decide how to test each characteristic, and work out a test programme
- decide how samples are to be selected, bought or otherwise obtained
- decide how the samples should be prepared for testing, including blanking out brand names and coding
- carry out a pilot test with a few samples to see whether the programme is practicable
- if necessary, revise the programme
- obtain all test samples
- make a list of all that you buy or acquire, noting details of each item
- carry out the test(s) according to the programme you have previously worked out, remembering the importance of controlled conditions
- analyse and examine test results
- prepare a draft report
- check the report, and repeat any tests where there are discrepancies
- prepare final report (see chapter 5)

The educational applications of comparative testing

People use the results of tests in consumer magazines – *Taenk, Que Choisir, Choice, Value, Test-Achats, Utusan Consumer, Which?* – to save themselves time and money. But they also learn something of longer term significance in that they begin to accept the process of comparison as something that can also be used in a variety of goods, services and situations. It is this educational aspect which appeals to teachers of all age groups and all subjects; but the scientific evaluation of one product or one service in relation to another is not something to be undertaken lightly – even if the subject seems simple, like ballpoint pens or toothpaste. It's easy to see what can be gained from comparative testing – training in critical awareness, in weighting and priority ranking, in reasoned, factually based decision making, in accuracy, logic, patience and objectivity, practice in different methods of clear presentation, and finally in report writing – all leading to a result which can be seen to have some point and be fun to achieve. It's not so easy to be aware in practice of all the possible pitfalls.

The educational problems

Organisation

Vast contemplations of checklists, flow charts and time and motion studies are likely to be needed once the choice of subject has been decided on – all things that can be guaranteed to keep you occupied in planning not just moderately past four o'clock but well into the night besides. Supplies have to be laid out and costed, equipment rounded up, facilities like running water and electric points checked on, the grouping and workload of the students dealt with – which means knowing interests and capabilities, understanding enmities and affinities and having in mind that child who, always having finished first, says 'what shall I do now, Miss?'

Time

It is difficult to estimate how long a comparative test will take. It may be that hours of intense preparation can barely sustain one 40 minute period of intense activity; or that you find you need a block of three periods demanding timetable switchings. Or your project may be ongoing, like a test for seed germination which transcends weekends and half terms and is subject to the mercies of caretakers, evening classes and Sunday schools.

Cost

This is now more likely than ever to influence the choice of the product to be tested. And the equipment for testing must already be available or makeshifts obvious. It is sad that you may have to reject some of the truly teenage orientated tests on crisps, cola drinks, yoghurts, and fast foods on the grounds of cost as well as of potential mess. It is of course possible to substitute observation tests. For example – at no cost at all – you could examine the premise that 'all brands of baked beans are just the same really': a simple study of their labels will soon suggest that this can't be so since ingredients vary, one brand containing milk and another vinegar.

Choice

What are the criteria for choosing a particular project in addition to cost?

- the subject should be relevant and of direct concern to students – and the younger the students the more this matters
- with luck the subject would originate from the students – like the examination of allegations that light bulbs last longer if they are used with the bulb facing downwards
- the point of the investigation should be clear, uncluttered and relatively limited. It is important not to mix up several kinds of test and to realise that some products are best tested for efficiency and others for value

Vigilance

Comparative testing is best avoided with a group that is known to be disruptive and noncooperative, unless you want repetitions of the performance of Paul who angrily jumped on six bags of potato crisps in quick succession because he would not record weights and contents before testing. But even with an orderly, reasonably predictable class, eagerness and competitiveness can also be counterproductive. Mary overwatered her batch of mustard and cress (instead of measuring out its daily 25 cc) because she wanted hers to grow fastest, and Tom snipped off the roots of Jeremy's onion so that it wouldn't grow at all. In addition to mishaps like these, you have to watch over every single measurement and recording that is made. And in a class exulting in something relatively new, you have to beware of equipment with potential but not necessarily obvious dangers – kettles of boiling water, bottles of bleach, scissors and packets of fertiliser.

Comparative tests to carry out

These low cost examples are on the face of it relatively simple, but they can be varied in depth and intensity according to the ability of the students you teach.

Example 1: germination rate of seeds
1 **Point of the investigation** To carry out a comparative test on the germination rate of different brands of seeds of one

particular kind (large seeds such as nasturtiums, beans, peas, marrows, melons, sunflowers).

2 **Characteristics of nasturtium seeds** Method of selling – in packets, in 'capsules'; number of seeds in a packet; cost per packet; where to buy them – specialist seed shops, chain stores, garden centres; instructions on packet; condition of seeds in packet; germination rate; quality of consequent plants; varieties and colours.

3 **Scope of the investigation** It is now necessary to decide which of these characteristics are important to you. If the enquiry is limited to germination rates, do you want to include purchase price and a final evaluation of value for money as well? Do you want to continue beyond germination and assess plants for colour and quality? If students themselves cannot go out to buy samples, does it matter what sort of a retail outlet the seeds came from, or could indeed their 'source' have a bearing on conditions of keeping and consequent germination?

4 **Cost** It is likely that there are about five commonly available brands of nasturtium seeds in different shops of different kinds in your neighbourhood, involving a relatively small outlay. In order to make sure that the packets you buy are typical of the batch they came from, you will have to buy more than one sample of each – in the first instance, two (a further sample could be necessary if you find that one of your collection is obviously defective in any way). Equipment for carrying out the tests should be available around school at no cost: ten (plus two for contingencies) identical seed boxes or substitutes such as egg boxes, poor sandy soil of consistent mix, sticks and labels for coding, measuring beaker for watering, paper and card for charts and grids. The total cost should not be enormous – and with any luck you should have enough plants to keep the school flower beds full of colour all summer.

5 **Order of operations**
   a code each packet in letters and numbers
   b draw up and duplicate two charts:
   Chart 1 will contain details (obtained from external observation of the packet) such as brand name, variety of nasturtium (e.g. Golden Gleam), type of plant (bush or climbing), where bought, price, instructions for planting, declared number of seeds (if any), reference to Seeds Act, and guarantee (if any)
   Chart 2 will contain details relating to contents of packet – number of seeds declared (if any), number of seeds found, general condition (on a five point scale from excellent to very poor)

   c having decided on the frequency of your observations, prepare a germination grid, bearing in mind that there is not likely to be any activity for the first week. Consider what 'germination' must mean for the purposes of this survey: it must relate to the first emergence of a shoot above ground
   d check that your paperwork is understandable, and that it is capable of being followed through by organising a trial run with a spare packet of seeds
   e having read the manufacturers' instructions – hoping that there won't be any great discrepancies of approach – plant the seeds, making sure that all have the same conditions of heat, light and water. Over four weeks record growth rate, in millimetres, of fully emergent plants
   f summary of findings and report writing, giving conclusions and possible value for money rating

Example 2: stain removal

1 **Point of the investigation** How is it best to remove school ink from white shirts and blouses? Is milk as a cleaning agent a myth?

2 **Equipment needed**
   a six squares of white blouse or shirt material, all the same size. These must be from the same (used) garment, perhaps salvaged from the school jumble sale, with equal amounts of wear. If, therefore, the pieces have to be small, they can be tacked for convenience on to a neutral, colourfast, backing material
   b standard school ink in an old eyedrop bottle or pipette
   c stain removers from the following – or your own – list: milk, bleach, lemon juice, soapless detergents of different brands, washing-up liquid; and appropriate amounts of hot and cold water
   d two sets of beakers (one for washing, one for rinsing) each with a stick-on label 1–6 or A–F on which the name of remover will be written. Since all these materials are readily available around school, no financial outlay should be involved (except perhaps for buying a lemon)

3 **Order of operations** Prepare charts on which to record findings. Prepare ink removers:
   a add 10 g of each detergent chosen to 100 cc of hot water
   b dilute bleach according to the manufacturers' instructions, repeating warnings about safety and possible effect of bleach on manmade fibres

Prepare stains – number each square with indelible ink and then place one drop of well mixed school ink in the centre of each.

4 **Action** Since it is important to do something at once with ink stains, do not wait for the ink to dry. Put square 1 into bowl 1 containing milk, square 2 into bowl 2 containing bleach, etc, square 6 into bowl 6 containing cold water. Leave materials to soak for 10 minutes, rinse them and then dry them at normal room temperatures. Evaluate the results, recording the effectiveness of various methods of ink removal: stain entirely removed, stain almost removed, some stain removed, stain left as it was originally. Which is the best method of 'first aid' treatment in school? *Does* ink come out best with milk?

5 **For further consideration** What would be the problems if ink had been spilled on grey Terylene and wool trousers or dress? What if the stain had been cocoa, blood or mud?

Example 3: yoyos
The example on page 88 shows the *results* of a test on yoyos which was carried out by students working with the American Consumers' Union. An experienced group can work backwards from someone else's findings, working out the tests that would need to be done.

List of other possibilities for comparative tests

shoe polish	ballpoint pens	washing-up liquids
soap	paper towels	window cleaning products
pencils	adhesives	bun and cake mixes
floor cleaners	bath salts	typewriter ribbons
erasers	shampoos	teenage magazines
fibre tipped pens	cameras	sticking plasters
construction kits	baby foods	torch batteries

Taste testing

Taste testing is a different kind of comparative testing, though many of the basic guidelines remain the same as those for other forms of survey work. Planning tools such as record charts, tables and questionnaires will be needed and must be tried out on a pilot scale first. The way in which you present samples must be standardised, with bowls and beakers made of nontaint material, and all of the same colour, size and shape. Lighting, humidity and temperature must all remain the same while the tests are going on. In addition, you must carefully scrutinise those actually doing the tasting – heavy smokers and people with colds are not going to be

KIDS TEST YO-YOS

Our testers found that all the yo-yos worked, but some were easier to handle than others. This chart lists the yo-yos in the order of how well the kids thought they worked. The ones they liked best are shown at the top of the chart. The first three — All-Star Champion, Duncan Imperial and Duncan Satellite — tied for first place. The last three — the Super-Hero, Human Bean and the butterfly-style Mickey Mouse Club models — tied for last place.

We've also listed the prices we paid for these Duncan and Festival yo-yos. Can you find the cheapest model for each company?

For Festival, the cheapest is the All-Star Champion. For Duncan, it's the Imperial. Where do these appear on the chart? Right at the top! Once again Penny Power toy-testers have found that "most expensive" doesn't always mean "best."

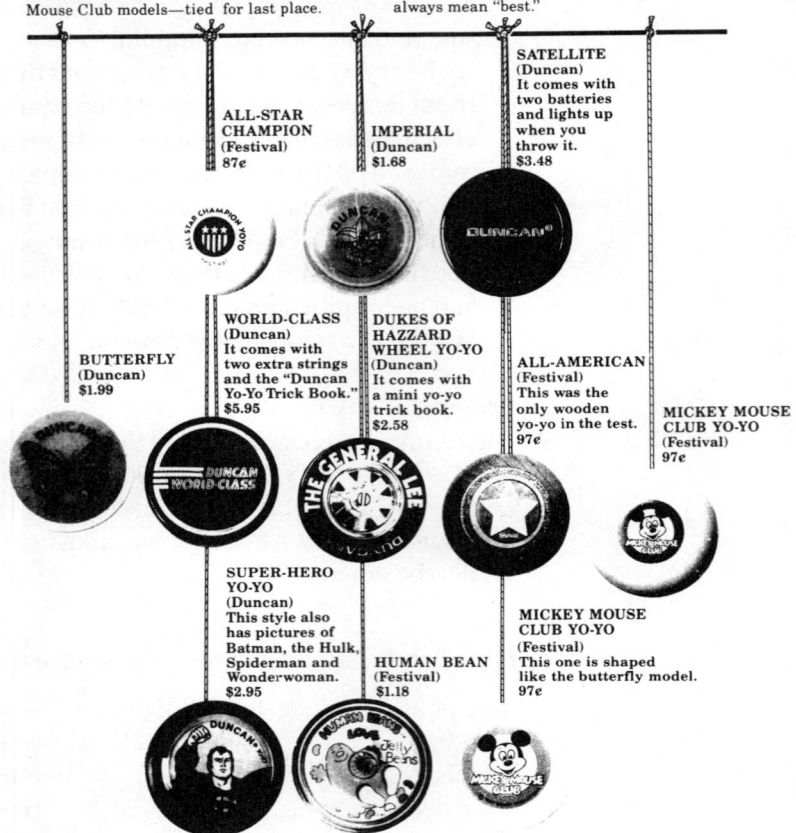

ALL-STAR CHAMPION (Festival) 87¢

IMPERIAL (Duncan) $1.68

SATELLITE (Duncan) It comes with two batteries and lights up when you throw it. $3.48

BUTTERFLY (Duncan) $1.99

WORLD-CLASS (Duncan) It comes with two extra strings and the "Duncan Yo-Yo Trick Book." $5.95

DUKES OF HAZZARD WHEEL YO-YO (Duncan) It comes with a mini yo-yo trick book. $2.58

ALL-AMERICAN (Festival) This was the only wooden yo-yo in the test. 97¢

MICKEY MOUSE CLUB YO-YO (Festival) 97¢

SUPER-HERO YO-YO (Duncan) This style also has pictures of Batman, the Hulk, Spiderman and Wonderwoman. $2.95

HUMAN BEAN (Festival) $1.18

MICKEY MOUSE CLUB YO-YO (Festival) This one is shaped like the butterfly model. 97¢

---

much use here. Taste tests matter very much to manufacturers – they carry out a lot of testing before they launch a new product to see whether most people will like it. Taste tests matter very much to consumers too – it is very important to be able to find the cheapest brand of food or drink that suits your taste.

There are several different kinds of taste test, with the choice in the case of a food manufacturer depending on the sort of information he requires. If, for example, a company wants to find out whether a new savoury yoghurt would fit into the existing market, then it would be likely to use a straightforward rating scale – which avoids putting people in the difficult position of having to describe flavours (or smells). Would they describe tea, as the Tea Council recommends, as 'pungent', 'malty' or 'brisk'?

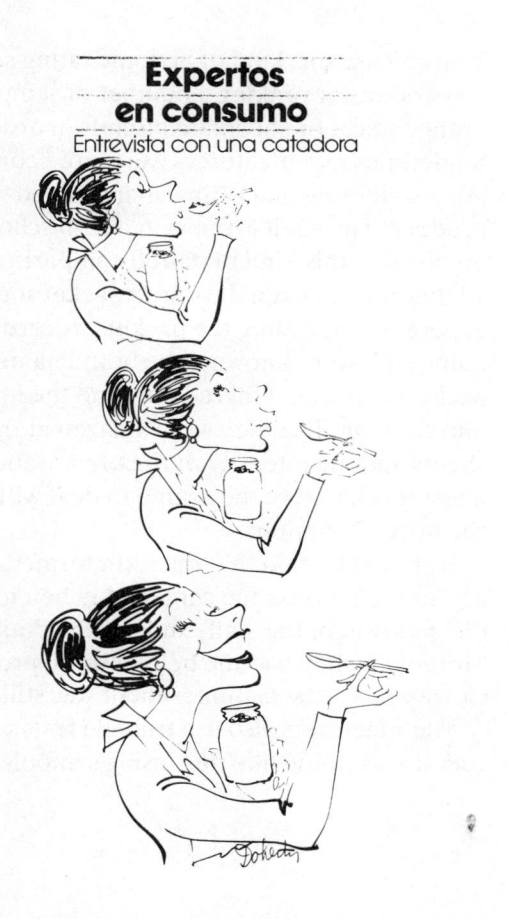

Expertos en consumo
Entrevista con una catadora

Most unlikely, but they would know the extent to which they liked or disliked it, especially if prompted by a rating chart. The following is an example of a rating chart:

9	like extremely
8	like very much
7	like moderately
6	like slightly
5	neither like nor dislike
4	dislike slightly
3	dislike moderately
2	dislike very much
1	dislike extremely

You can use this kind of hedonic rating scale easily in the classroom, for ranking a number of samples of hamburgers, orange juice, or chocolate biscuits in order of preference. Sometimes manufacturers use paired comparison tests when they are considering marketing an improved version of an established product. The sixth formers at a high school in Bedfordshire were involved in this kind of paired comparison test, which dealt with 19 different chicken flavoured packet soups. They appreciated the experience of coding the packets, recording the manufacturer's name (if it were known), the brand name, the quantity in the pack, the listing of ingredients and the instructions for preparation and cooking. But they were amazed at the number of record sheets and the intensity of the organisation required to set up such a test, even before they came to deal with the final form used for the tasters' opinions.

It should be said that the sixth formers conducting this taste test had to monopolise the canteen kitchen for a whole morning, with the goodwill of the staff, and use the dining room for their tests. Moreover, they had the help of three project officers from the Consumers' Association – and it was still a difficult enterprise.

Manufacturers also use triangle tests where three samples are coded something like this, using symbols:

□   ○   ◇

Two of the samples are alike and one is different, and it is the task of the taster to indicate the one which is different. Can you tell Stork from butter? Can you pick out the Kelloggs cornflakes from own brand flakes? Can you detect the homemade scones from those made from a packet mix? This is a difficult test in the classroom or college unless there is a specialised department of food science; it not only puts heavy demands on the teacher, and is likely to be costly, but it also provides students designated as testers with far more work to do than the tasters, who have instant fun but soon get bored. The only solution here is to run two parallel taste tests so that tasters and testers get a turn at both jobs. But two tests increase the demands on time, organisation and money; this is best left alone under normal school circumstances. There is even a duo/trio test where the taster is provided with a known reference sample together with two unknown samples, one of which is the same as the reference sample. Here the taster has to decide which of the unknown samples is the same as the reference sample. This is again to be noted and left to the specialist.

Cream of chicken soup - taste test

User name _____ User no _____ Date _____

You should taste the two bowls of soup we give you, and then fill in this form. We ask you about several things which apply to how soup tastes. We have given soup △ a score of 5 for all these aspects and we want you to compare soup ○ with soup △. You may not be able to distinguish between soup △ and soup ○ - don't worry about this, just give ○ a score of 5.

Please tick the appropriate boxes (✓). Remember soup △ is always scored 5.

```
                    Soup △
              0 1 2 3 4 5 6 7 8 9 10
```

Q1	What score would you give soup ○ for *strength of flavour*?	much weaker	☐☐☐☐☐|☐|☐☐☐☐☐	much stronger (30)
Q2	What score would you give soup ○ for its *amount of seasoning*?	much less seasoned	☐☐☐☐☐|☐|☐☐☐☐☐	much more seasoned (31)
Q3	What score would you give soup ○ for its *creaminess*?	much less creamy	☐☐☐☐☐|☐|☐☐☐☐☐	much creamier (32)
Q4	What score would you give soup ○ for *smoothness*?	much less smooth	☐☐☐☐☐|☐|☐☐☐☐☐	much smoother (33)
Q5	What score would you give soup ○ for *saltiness*?	much less salty	☐☐☐☐☐|☐|☐☐☐☐☐	much saltier (34)
Q6	What score would you give soup ○ for being *glutinous*?	less glutinous	☐☐☐☐☐|☐|☐☐☐☐☐	more glutinous (35)
Q7	What score would you give soup ○ for its *bits of chicken*?	less bits of chicken	☐☐☐☐☐|☐|☐☐☐☐☐	more bits of chicken (36)
Q8	What score would you give soup ○ for *tasting of chicken*?	tastes less of chicken	☐☐☐☐☐|☐|☐☐☐☐☐	tastes more like chicken (37)
Q9	What score would you give soup ○ for being *good quality*?	worse quality	☐☐☐☐☐|☐|☐☐☐☐☐	better quality (38)

Q10 What would you say was the predominant flavour of soup ○ ? *Please write in:* (39)

(40)

Q11 Have you any other comments to make about soup ○ ? *Please write in:* (41)

(42)

Simple scientific tests

Teachers of nonscientific subjects can be faced with a scientific test as part of the logical process of carrying out a project in social or business studies – maybe as a direct result of student demand. You are likely to feel daunted and to question whether the inclusion of such tests is worth while.

What is the point of an 'integrated' scientific test?

- It can add to the range of skills – accuracy, assessment, evaluation, objectivity.
- It gives the chance to those students who haven't been able to do science to have a brief insight into scientific methods of testing and analysis.
- It provides a more varied input to the project, introducing an entirely different set of approaches and concepts.
- It helps students to understand the problems related to marketing and promotion, advertising, packaging and labelling, mass production, quality control, pricing policies and even to the morality of making claims about a product. Take, for example, the students at Suan Sunandha College of Education in Bangkok, Thailand. As part of a general studies project on traditional and modern medicines, they analysed one of South East Asia's best known panaceas, which will 'cure' anything from mosquito bites to a sprained ankle. They looked at marketing strategies, packaging and promotion and decided that the product was overpriced. So they went into business within the college campus, selling their cream in clear glass jars for eye appeal, and making a modest profit.
- It helps students to understand and take part in the solution of social – as well as commercial – problems. Take another example from a developing country. In India, where food adulteration is one of the greatest dangers, students are able to find out whether the things they eat are contaminated. It is easy enough to discover by nonchemical tests if there is sand or talcum in sago – pure sago swells when it is burnt and leaves hardly any ash. If tea is 'second hand' and artificially coloured it leaves spots of pink, red or yellow on a sheet of wet paper. If grass seeds are disguised as cumin seeds, then the black charcoal rubs off in your fingers. But it is *chemical* tests that are needed to detect the really lethal adulterants. Cooking oil can be contaminated by highly poisonous argemone oil, which is detected by adding a solution of hydrochloric acid and ferric chloride which causes the argemone to turn reddish brown. Turmeric, used in curries, can contain metanil yellow – discovered by adding concentrated hydrochloric acid to a solution of the powder, which turns red when the solution is

then diluted with water. Sugar can contain washing soda which effervesces in hydrochloric acid, or turns red litmus blue if it is dissolved in water. The fact that such tests are now being used in and out of school by nonspecialists is beginning to have a disciplinary effect on unscrupulous or ignorant traders who can poison, paralyse and even kill thousands of people with one batch of an adulterated product. The International Organisation of Consumers' Unions sends out – for distribution by consumer organisations – a kit containing these essential chemicals, simple instructions and a colour chart to help in the identification of particular poisons.

What are the problems for nonspecialists in carrying out such tests?

- A simple subject can turn out to need test methods which are far from simple.
- Products needed for testing may have to be bought out of an already inadequate budget.
- School equipment may be limited, as a Scottish school doing an investigation into the effectiveness of common household glues on solid materials found out: 'We suggested our own methods rather than the procedures outlined in various books, because we were restricted by limited apparatus and we wanted to consider the properties of the glues from a household point of view. Originally we tried using clothes pegs, sticking the two flat surfaces together, but the surface of the joint turned out to be too large, and the force required to break the joint was beyond the limits of our equipment.'
- Other people's laboratory accommodation, equipment and expertise will be needed.
- Testing arrangements – for the specialist as well as the nonspecialist – can be unpredictable, as a Hertfordshire school discovered in its tests on yoghurt: 'The tests were all to be carried out in the science lab, but owing to a gas leak which made the bunsen burners out of order we had to boil (*sic*) samples on an electric stove in the cooking room.'
- Tests have to be devised – to find out how long soap will last, how well it kills off the 'bactria in our bodies', how homemade soap can be produced: 'We got two beakers and labelled them A and B. In beaker A we put:

    6 g stearic acid
    2 g cocunut oil
    1 g olive oil

In beaker B we put:

8 g water
3 g sodium hydroxide
1.4 g potassium hydroxide
2 g gycrine

Then we heated them both to 75°. After that we poured beaker B gradualy into beaker A and stiring it constantly until cool. We left it for 48 hours.'
- Dangerous chemicals may have to be used – as in the case of the tests for food adulterants.

If there isn't willing specialist support, then it is unwise to start off on any scientific test. With such support, students can help themselves by looking at the methods used by consumer organisations and by writing to manufacturers: 'First we wrote to Lever Brothers Ltd, Colgate Palmolive Ltd and Proctor and Gambole Ltd asking for technichal information and display material.'

Investigating and inquiring

There is no single prototype for a project – which is the cause of difficulties for teachers in charge of plans and preparations. Some projects will include techniques such as testing, questioning and interviewing; others will adopt a different approach entirely, tied in with the final medium or method of presentation. In many cases the components of a project depend on the subject chosen and on the timetable available. Moreover, if there is a relatively free choice of subject, which can often be possible even within the framework of an examination syllabus, the starting point is likely to be a local or regional issue, need or problem, sometimes with national implications – but with the known and familiar community still at its heart.

Local and community projects

Example 1: telephone kiosks
'The telephone boxes on our estate are always out of order when we want to ring up our boyfriends.'

'My Mum, she was going to have a baby and the pains came on bad and she sent me to telephone the hospital. But the phone wouldn't work so I ran all the way to the doctor.'

Irritation and indignation. What was the truth of the matter? How many telephones were actually out of order? Since this was an unscheduled project sparked off by strong personal feelings and consequent emotions, only three separate afternoons could be set aside – one for planning and preparing, the second for carrying out their inquiry, and the third for writing it up and considering future action. The girls got a complete list of telephone kiosks ('But what if there are any of those funny new phones?') in the area from the post office, marked their positions on a local street plan in red ink, visited the three nearest boxes to get some idea of the sort of questions they ought to be seeking to answer, and then designed a checklist (which they typed out and duplicated) of items to note or tests to carry out:

- Is the box a standard coin box?
- Is there a London directory? Are any pages missing?
- Are there any local directories – and the *Yellow Pages*?
- Are dialling code lists available?
- Are there emergency instructions telling you where the phone is? (they considered this information necessary for strangers to their area)
- Is there any damage to the phone, coin box, lighting, kiosk itself?
- Is the telephone clean?
- Is the telephone in working order?

When they came to write up their findings on the thirty-five kiosks they had looked at – seven each for five girls – they did in fact find some of the phones out of order, but certainly not all, and they recognised that the fault lay in public misuse and vandalism. 'That kiosk at Tudor Hill was really filthy, there were two cracked windows, the dialling codes was gone, it smelt horrible, it was stuffy; it was littered with bits of paper, dirt, cigarette packets and worse.' They found an example of a design fault where the electric cable was trapped when the door of the kiosk closed, which they reported to British Telecom. They decided to go back a week later to find out if repairs had been carried out. This error cheered them up somewhat, because they had proved themselves wrong – that the phones weren't *always* out of order, and that even when they were it was more often than not the public's own fault and not that of the industry. 'The problem's changed, Miss – it's not the phones, it's the people we need to think about now.'

The cartoon from Malaysia on page 96 shows that telephone problems are not confined to south west Hertfordshire alone.

Example 2: shop safety and toys at Christmas
A mixed group of 13–15 year-olds, investigating public awareness of fire risk in public places, interviewed shoppers in the centre of

PUBLIC telephones are probably the only means of telecommunication facilities for the vast majority of people in Malaysia.

They are thus very necessary both in the urban as well as in the rural areas but especially in places where few subscriber telephones are installed. In places like these, the existence or non-existence of a public telephone may be a matter of life and death.

In urban areas, public telephones are needed to cater to the large floating population and also in the many large housing estates that are rapidly coming up because of the rapid rate of urbanisation in the country.

In the rural areas where the transportation network is not very well developed, and no alternate modes of communication are available, the public telephone becomes an indispensable aid in maintaining links with other places. Provision of public telephones in such settlements and villages should be given top priority by the Telecoms Department.

There is no lack of complaints about delays by the Telecoms Department in installing public phones, especially from villages, as shown in the cases below....

Strasbourg. They used a questionnaire, reproduced on page 69–70, to guide them in finding out what people thought about safety precautions in two stores in the same part of the city – one modern and one less recently built. They carried out their survey on a Thursday afternoon between 3 and 5 o'clock when the traffic was fairly heavy; this was important in assessing how long it would take for the fire brigade to arrive. Surprisingly, only 55% of the total sample expected it to arrive in five minutes or less. The students found that most people did not seem to be very worried about the adequacy of safety precautions, even though a large majority had no idea what measures actually existed. Women especially thought they might panic in the event of a fire. The students' findings appeared in the regional newspaper, alerting shoppers as well as shops to the need to be concerned about fire risks.

The same school, as part of an ongoing series of projects, investigated buying toys at Christmas. They found that the real problem in finding suitable toys for children lay in the choices made by consumers who were not the final users. What do adults look for when they are buying a toy as a present? The students carried out a survey, asking nearly 1000 people why they had chosen a particular toy for their child: 30% bought it because the child had asked for it, 19% because of its educational value, 13% because price was the first consideration, just over 4% because they liked it themselves, and just over 1% because they had seen an advertisement.

They went on to compare prices of toys in different shops, to find out why people went to one shop rather than another, to discover how much families planned to spend on toys at Christmas time. These results too were published in *Dernières Nouvelles d'Alsace*, but in addition they turned their project into an audiovisual presentation. They produced a set of 160 slides – of photographs, cartoons, tables and diagrams – and a 50 minute commentary in the form of a dialogue between two of the students.

Example 3: supermarket shopping
Severely mentally handicapped students with varying physical handicaps carried out this project in inner London as part of a two year 'Gateway' course. The point of their project was to enable them to become as independent as possible, and to do this their college needed the help of the community – in this case, the cooperation of the local Safeways supermarket. Rosie, for example, takes her work card to Albert so that he can help her do her shopping: 'Please will you give Rosie two rashers of back

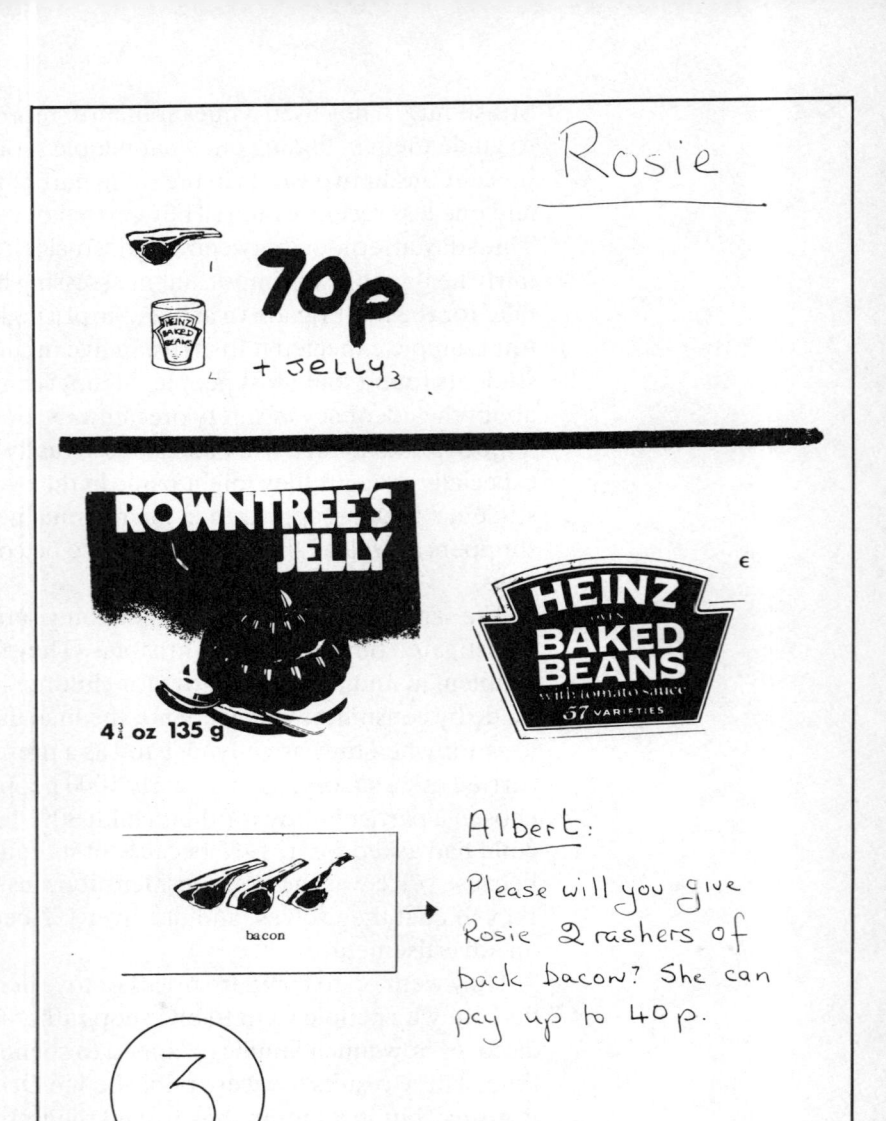

> Rosie
>
> 70p
> + jelly₃
>
> ———————————
>
> **ROWNTREE'S JELLY** 4¾ oz 135 g
>
> **HEINZ BAKED BEANS** with tomato sauce 57 VARIETIES
>
> bacon → Albert:
> Please will you give Rosie 2 rashers of back bacon? She can pay up to 40p.
>
> ③ ✶✶✶

bacon?' Rosie can't read at all but she knows she likes beans, bacon and jelly – three things. The picture on her card is there to remind her. She can just about recognise the number 3 and link it to the three stars at the bottom of the page. So Rosie goes to Safeways and proudly spends her 70p. In general, the various stages of this regularly repeated project are:

- group discussion on menu choices (illustrated on page 99)
- individual students count out their money
- students make a guided choice and a shopping list 'written' according to ability

```
SAMPLE MENU CHOICES

① ?                              ② ?
  new potatoes                     oven chips
  fruit salad                       ?
  (40p to spend)                   (70p to spend)

③ ?                              ④ ?
  Rice — plain ?                   pasta — noodles ?
       OR                               OR
        \ curried ?                    \ spaghetti ?
  fruit in jelly                   yoghurt or piece
                                   of fruit
  (40p to spend)                   (50p to spend)

⑤ ?                              ⑥ ?
  instant potato                   jacket potato
  cheesecake or desert             sponge pudding
              whip                 and custard
  (60p to spend)                   (30p to spend)
  between 2
```

- students go shopping, knowing to ask the assistants for any necessary help
- cashier checks the students' cards to see that they have bought the right things within their budget
- cashier takes the students' money, explains the change and gives a receipt
- back at college the students 'explain' their purchases and their change

Controversy in the community

Some projects deal with sensitive or controversial subjects like racial issues, conflicts between town and country dwellers, the choice of site for a new airport, motorway or power station, the

99

problem of the need for employment and the desire to preserve the environment. The following examples deal in some detail with two 'difficult' subjects. Should students avoid subjects like travellers and mental handicap? To avoid controversy is to avoid life.

Example 1: travellers
'The children go to school but they don't learn much – only laziness.'
'Travelling children were stuck in one class and just done more or less what they wanted to.'

These were comments made by two travellers to a group of fifth formers as part of their social education project. The travellers, who were busy picking potatoes, talked freely to the students because there was a personal bond and a common interest. One of the students was keen on boxing and had boxed against one of the sons of a local traveller family; but, after an incident at a contest, the family was banned from attending future matches and the boy from boxing in public. The other students were curious to know more about a family and a lifestyle which were totally unfamiliar to them, and so the idea of a project developed, to be based on interviews which would lead on to a slide/tape presentation to develop a better understanding of the travellers' point of view – not just in school but in the community.

It was a daring idea with an unpredictable outcome. Would the travellers be resentful, feeling that there was an intrusion into their privacy? Would they feel that the students were superior and patronising? What would the attitude of the local authority be, since the travellers were known to be causing environmental problems as they dealt in old cars and scrap metal? Would social service departments take exception to interference by inexperienced students? After a rather difficult start, the problems implicit in these questions did not develop, largely because it soon became obvious that the students had won the confidence of the travellers; they were happy to talk to young people, who were no threat to them, about family life, education and work. Moreover, it was not the intention of the students to make any sort of judgment in their project, merely to record and give shape to what they were told. And they were able to include in their final presentation interviews with professional social workers who knew that their comments would be played back to their 'clients'.

Example 2: helping the handicapped
'It's just like Colditz' was the reaction of a group of CSE social studies students confronted with Leavesden Hospital, which looks

after the mentally handicapped. They hadn't really wanted to go, but were attracted against their will for two reasons: they were going to get out of school for the whole of every Thursday afternoon, and they had seen Leavesden Hospital on TV as the setting for the popular series about prison life called 'Porridge' – doing a stretch. After all, they might even see Ronnie Barker in action. The hospital is an enormous place, solidly Victorian, built as the Victorians built all their schools, hospitals and prisons, and set in large, attractive grounds with trees and gardens and a pets' corner with an incredibly large but docile sheep as its dominant inhabitant, much loved by the patients. Pets' corner was all right as part of the preliminary visit, but the buildings and the inmates came as a shock – the mixed smells of disinfectant, vomit and urine, the patients who drooled and dribbled, the pathos of tiny children with shrunken limbs, deformities and outsize heads. Still, no one was being made to go, so they might as well give their project a try.

The basic intention was to find out how well the mentally handicapped were catered for in Hertfordshire within the context of the National Health Service. The project came about because some of the teachers involved in social studies had direct contacts with the staff of the hospital, which was very short of volunteer visitors, particularly for patients who had no relatives: some had been put in hospital half a century ago as a punishment for some youthful misdemeanour, and were still there. The teachers were also aware that they too had some problem students, not very bright, inadequate and sometimes themselves deprived of affection and relationships. Could these two disparate groups be put together to obtain mutual and lasting satisfaction – as well as produce some sort of CSE report with a format as yet unspecified?

The idea was to make a study of mental health, state provisions for it and community attitudes towards it. The officers at the hospital with whom the project was discussed felt that the students should also learn how a large institution functions (how it is organised, how thousands of meals are prepared, how countless socks and shirts are laundered, how unpleasantly soiled linen is dealt with, how ancillary services like dentistry, chiropody and hairdressing are arranged), how such a hospital fits into the general scheme of health care, and how the attitudes of the staff and their backgrounds influenced the way they saw their roles. So the project had a general (and ultimately examinable) aim, but its structure was always flexible so that if difficulties arose and were insurmountable they could be bypassed. One such difficulty arose early on when one group of five boys saw an overworked charge nurse struggling to distribute meals to a large ward. The boys did not know that the nurse was on his own because of a labour dispute, and they never really did understand why their head teacher received a stern letter of reproach from the trade union. They were sad not to be able to flip fried eggs on to a plate any more or even scrape up the waste for the pig bin.

Reluctant students soon developed commitment to their hospital and the patients they adopted. They learned to ignore the unpleasanter physical side of handicap and they were quite happy to play children's games and chat, infinitely repeating the same thing, or communicate quite meaningfully with nods and grunts. They could even help with some basic skills. Norma from the Caribbean desperately wanted to be able to tie her own shoelaces, and her visitors carefully made a large cardboard model with eyelet holes and thick string – it was rather clumsy but it was effective as a teaching aid and Norma loved it. They promised her a whole packet of her favourite ginger biscuits when she could tie her laces all by herself. But one Thursday when they clattered noisily into Norma's ward she was not there. Norma had died. 'She'll never know how to do her shoes up now.' It was their first experience with sudden death, and the death of somebody who was not much older than they were. This was a new situation for the teachers in charge of the project to deal with, a discussion of the extremity of 'it's not fair, Miss'; but they were able to come to terms with death by their school's acceptance of their request to go to Norma's funeral in school time. They were clean and soberly dressed and they took flowers for the lonely coffin – but they brought them away from the crematorium afterwards and put them in Norma's ward. This was their first death and they grew to know when it was becoming imminent in older friends, even to hold hands with the dying, even to promise that seventy-year-old Annie should have her teddybear buried with her.

But it was the living, in their resilience, that they cared for, and their caring caused problems. Thursday afternoons in school time were supervised with a fairly high ratio of teachers, but some students started to call in during the evenings and others turned up on a Saturday – when there was a dreadful occasion on which they decided to organise an unofficial wheelchair race. Production of a project report also caused problems: they were profiting from stable relationships with patients and from being regarded as people of significance, they were learning new skills and new qualities such as patience, perseverance and tolerance, but they were very loth to put anything down on paper. They were gently nagged into doing drawings with brief descriptions, designing simple aids like Norma's shoelace gadget, and making tape recordings, and Patrick was finally moved to write a poem about

Colditz. Keeping a diary turned out to be relatively acceptable, and they were able in many cases to produce records of progress with regard to health and the acquisition of skills.

A similar study, possibly even simultaneous, was carried out at the other side of the world in Victoria, Australia, where students' reaction to a project on the Mayday Hills Hospital was very much the same as that of the Hertfordshire children: 'Make a study of the mental institution in our town!' Together the two investigations produce useful guidelines for any project, and particularly one with an element of controversy, within the community:

- It is essential to have a key reference person actually in the institution who understands the purpose of the project, who is willing to give authoritative information in a clear and sympathetic way, and who is compatible with the students.
- In the event of any difficulty with trade unions or hospital staff, this liaison officer must be available for immediate contact.
- A high ratio of staff to students is needed so that they can be divided into small groups with specific tasks that are seen to be useful.
- The possibility of a substantial dropout rate has to be faced, since making someone work in a mental hospital against his will is not going to serve any useful function; and if there is a high dropout rate alternative plans have to be made – perhaps a parallel activity in local nursery schools.
- The rationalisation of out-of-school activity has to be faced (even the attendance at funerals and parental reaction to their children's exposure to death), without inhibiting the development of genuine caring.
- Lists of students must be available for checking in and out at the beginning and end of each session, so that teachers and supervisors know exactly who is doing what and where he is doing it.
- Rearrangement of the timetable must permit a three period block, preferably an afternoon, for any community activity.

Possibilities for projects

1. Collecting facts about the past and present state of the institution and its setting (in the case of Leavesden, vast opportunities were present since the archives contain records of costs, admissions, discharges, diseases and deaths since the mid 1840s).
2. Finding out what people think – in other words, carrying out a survey to determine public attitudes, and even the attitudes of the staff to the patients they care for and the general situation

regarding mental health. A questionnaire could be tactfully designed or interviews structured to find out from the staff what problems the hospital faced, what changes were needed, what were the priorities in finance, staffing and facilities, the role of drug therapy, and what they felt about the influence and impact of the institution on the community. The Australian survey was not, in fact, successful because the staff were on the defensive. Nevertheless the students – as their teacher said – 'were jolted into understanding that mental health was a controversial issue', and realised the need for extreme diplomacy in carrying out any investigation in an institution where public servants may not necessarily be free to make statements.

3   Systematic discussions in small working groups of students, and discussions between students, community groups and the institution's staff.
4   Keeping of careful records and progress reports, perhaps in the form of a diary or numbered photographs, if these are allowed, even the development of case histories.
5   Investigating the cost of keeping a patient in a mental hospital and the alternatives of sheltered housing and community care.
6   Designing simple products or seeing existing ones with new eyes – like bending a cheap spoon handle so that an old lady with crippled fingers could feed herself, or covering a tray with green baize Fablon so that plates did not slip for bedfast patients.

Economic and social projects

In a number of developing countries, project work is essentially functional and tied in with the social and economic needs of the country. In Kenya, at Elemit (see opposite), the students helped to build their own school. In Jamaica, the network of literacy centres across the island publishes booklets with simple illustrations and diagrams on how to keep a pig, goat or rabbit, with guidance on building a shelter and keeping accounts. In India, the Trusteeship Foundation in Bombay gives detailed help on similar projects which are particularly useful to unemployed young people. Nor is it unknown for rural schools in the United Kingdom to be involved in the care and costing of projects on gardening or looking after animals. Class 4b from chapter 3 went in for cultivating a small patch of garden: they decided to grow *nicotiana* – attractive looking plants that have beautiful, sweet scented flowers but that do actually produce tobacco leaves. They carefully costed their seeds and fertiliser, worked out how much they were going to save producing their own cigarettes, and looked at Customs & Excise regulations. But their project came to

A 'do-it-yourself' school in Elemit, Kenya, built by the community with the help of children

nothing – apart from a good display of flowers – because someone watered the leaves at the drying stage and mould destroyed the entire crop. Other European projects turn out to be more innocent and more successful, increasingly having the advantage of linking up school and adult life: even a small rural school in the Isère valley in France, very much concerned to find additional uses for increasing milk yields and apple production, became involved in the development of new products and marketing methods. Such projects fit in well with commerce, business studies and social studies wherever they exist, because they are real and they involve a variety of lifelong skills. The first project on keeping a goat outlined below comes from Maharashtra, but apart from the prices, which are given in rupees (still using the old British shilling sign with about 17 to £1 sterling), the ideas could be applicable anywhere and could be expanded into a cooperative enterprise.

Example 1: keeping a goat – a model scheme with three goats for two years
Investment cost
Purchase of 3 does @ 200/– each   600/–
Shed   100/–

Operative cost

Concentrates @ 250 g per goat per day, 3 goats, 2 years	655/–
Concentrates @ 100 g per kid per day, 14 kids, 120 days	200/–
Green fodder @ 3 kg per goat per day, 3 goats, 2 years	525/–
Green fodder @ 2 kg per kid per day, 14 kids, 120 days	269/–
Dry fodder @ 500 g per goat per day, 3 goats, 2 years	330/–
Dry fodder @ 200 g per kid per day, 14 kids, 120 days	102/–
Miscellaneous contingencies	50/–
Interest on total capital, say 2900/– @ 12%	348/–
For one unit, say 2480 rupees	2479/–

Receipts

4 kiddings in 2 years will give say 16 kids (8 male and 8 female); expectation that 2 will die (10%).

Sale of 14 kids at 6 months @ 100/– each	1400/–
Skins of 2 dead kids @ 10/–	20/–
Milk yield (1 litre per goat per day)	1800/–
8 cart loads of manure in 2 years @ 30/–	240/–
	3460/–

Profit

Gross receipt	3460/–
Operative cost	2480/–
Net profit	980/–

The net profit on one unit, that is three goats and their offspring, is 980/– over two years.

These are the figures provided by the Integrated Rural Development Programme in Bombay. It can be seen that no allowance has been made for depreciation of the initial investment and that, given the flow of receipts, the capital borrowing is rather high. Nevertheless, the general project idea remains sound, and interesting facts are revealed – that 10% of kids die, that an adult goat produces 1 litre of milk a day, that a small group of goats produces 8 cart loads of manure in two years.

Example 2: keeping a dog
'Miss, I gotta dog.' Peter never said very much at school though he did a great deal that was disturbing and disruptive. Where had he got his dog from? Had he stolen it, the others wanted to know with some curiosity? And they moved on to develop 'Peter's dog' into a project – though they never called it a project, always referring to it as 'doing Peter's dog'. They looked at the best ways of buying a dog, or any pet for that matter, what to look for, how to evaluate the animal's needs and the owner's responsibilities. What does a dog eat if he's properly fed? How much does his food cost? What are the comparative prices of tinned food or fresh dog meat? What other costs are involved in petkeeping? What about a licence, the vet's fees, injections? What about legal responsibilities in keeping pets? What about the need to care for something – not just a dog, but as the others admitted, perhaps a ferret down the garden or three snails in a saucer?

The possibility of pets as a project is not new, though there is more emphasis now on this psychological value of keeping pets – people who have a pet live longer and suffer less from stress, which students can check up on in a survey. There is also more emphasis on the justification for feeding an animal expensively when two-thirds of the world is either suffering from malnutrition or actually starving. There is also the invasion by commerce of the pet world, advancing far beyond initial purchase and provision of basic needs and services into poodle parlours, special clothes, funerals, even special cards 'from your cat to our cat'. Is the encouragement of a pet as a status symbol, its elevation to that of a replacement human being, a moral commercial aim? All these issues can be explored as part of a project, but the most relevant is that of the cost of keeping an animal. Only when you know the real cost can you balance out whether the advantages of ownership outweigh its disadvantages. The cost may be prohibitive. The 'Peter's dog' project which arose spontaneously on the first occasion has been refined over the years within the framework of social studies and commerce, sometimes working in conjunction with the maths department, and capable of being adapted to the needs of students with wide ranging abilities.

Certainly with CSE students it is wise to accept that they will have little idea in the first place of the difference between capital outlay and running costs (or what the 'goat' enterprise calls investment and operative costs). Left to themselves they mix up cans of pet food, pounds of liver and lights, dog baskets, vets' fees, boarding kennels, licences together with the original cost of the animal. By brainstorming they can produce a long list of many different kinds of cost, and then be prodded into the discovery that there are two main sorts – those which occur only once, and those that go on taking place week after week. The capital costs of the dog, its basket, blanket, food bowls, its first round of distemper injections are all easy to group. 'But what if he breaks his bowl or chews up his blanket?' So, apart from the animal itself, capital costs are not once-and-for-all – depreciation (and the analogy with cars and motorbikes is useful here) has to be taken into account. The operative costs are not clear cut, either: students can find out with some certainty how much it costs to feed a dog and give it its vitamins each week, but there is much less predictability over amounts for vets' services or worming tablets, holiday boarding kennels, or presents to the neighbour who looks after the dog. But the costs will vary enormously – which doesn't mean to say that any of them are wrong – because of the difference in expectation of life of breed of dog and the way in which people choose to spend their money on it. But there is at the very least an answer to the question, 'Can we afford to keep a dog?', because there is a definable minimum. But whether a family can afford even this minimum if Dad loses his job remains an open question. Psychologically the dog might be even more necessary.

Giving guidelines: stimulus materials

What do you do with a student who says, 'I don't know what to do'? Such a comment is not uncommon, nor does it always come from less able students: it may be that the demands of mixed ability teaching are too great, time too short or staffing ratios inadequate for the explanations and supervision that project based learning often requires. In such a situation the answer is to look for strategies which arouse and maintain interest, and provide an acceptable framework for action without restricting freedom and initiative. Just as there is no single format for a project, so there is no single strategy: multiple and varied approaches have to be available. You can prepare some of these in advance (sometimes well in advance so long as they are regularly reviewed and updated), and use them as part of an emergency stockpile on general interest topics.

The following suggestions, which don't include commercially available materials, do not set out to form an exhaustive list. Their function is to provide practical guidance based on experience, and to spark off other ideas and possible methods of approach. Some of the strategies and techniques will fail with a given group, but this doesn't mean that they will fail with a different group; nor does one success mean a progression and proliferation of further successes. Supervision leads to the detection of a trend, right or wrong, and – if necessary – to a change of tactic.

Outline plans and possibilities

You can duplicate such plans, breaking down a fairly general subject into sections each of which can stand on its own. Then split each section in turn into paragraph headings with suggestions for activities following on from these headings.

Example 1: the economic system

Topic	Content	Activity
The consumer and his role in the market economy	Definition of a consumer Consumer income and expenditure Distribution of income and wealth Social changes that affect the market Consumer interest and consumer sovereignty	1 Complete the questionnaire: 'What do you think?' 2 Discuss how teenage spending habits affect the economy. 3 Discuss or debate whether consumer demand dictates the packaging of a product or whether the package is the result of what the manufacturer thinks the consumer wants. 4 List products you think are overpackaged and collect/display examples.
The purpose of an economy	What should we produce? How much? and for whom? Consumption directed economy versus consumer directed economy	Compare a free enterprise consumer directed economy such as Australia or the UK with the government regulated economy of China or Russia. The conditions necessary for a consumer directed economy are *a* competition, *b* reasonable distribution of income, *c* a public sector which provides services, *d* informed consumers who know their rights and responsibilities. Discuss why each is necessary and what happens if any one is eliminated.
The producer–retailer–consumer relationship	What it is What it can be The difficult role of the consumer	Devise a role play (or write a radio script) about a problem between buyer and seller (e.g. shoes allegedly sold as leather turning out to be plastic). Discuss whether each 'side' understood its rights and responsibilities. Discuss the difference between what an economist means by 'economy' and what the man in the street thinks it means. Carry out a simple survey to find out what people do think.

What makes the economy function? (legal, social and commercial aspects – see illustration below)

Supply and demand
Inflation and deflation
Pricing and price control
Technological advances
International forces
Competition – its role, conditions necessary for its function, its control
Reductions and rebates
Monopolies, oligopolies and exclusive concessions
Commercial and industrial history
Misuse of economic power

Use the circular flow model to help you describe the functioning of the market.
Discuss the meaning of inflation and the use of the retail price index.
Discuss current economic problems such as productivity, unemployment, the monetary system. Use the flow model to trace breakdowns in the cycle which lead to inflation and recession.
Make a list of ways in which consumers are affected by ups and downs in the economy.
How can consumers protect themselves? What is the consumer's role in maintaining a balanced economy?
Make a list of public and private monopolies, and show the effect of one of them on the free enterprise system.

The circular flow model

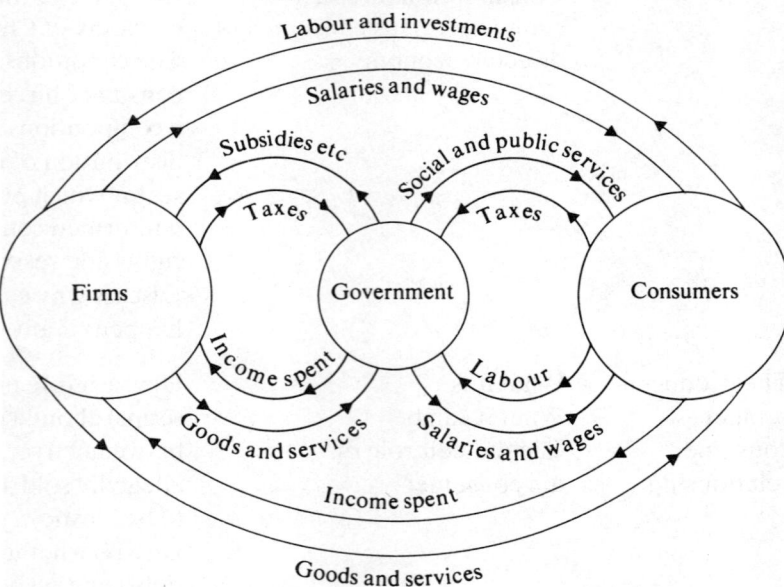

(Diagram: Three circles labelled Firms, Government, and Consumers, connected by flows labelled: Labour and investments, Salaries and wages, Subsidies etc, Social and public services, Taxes, Taxes, Income spent, Labour, Goods and services, Salaries and wages, Income spent, Goods and services)

This example, which has been adapted from one published for Australian schools by the Consumer Affairs Bureau in the Department of the Capital Territory, is suitable for general as well as specific use within commerce, economics or business studies classes.

As a consumer, what do you think?

Read each statement carefully and tick the box which most accurately describes your opinion about it.

	Agree	Disagree	Don't Know
1 Consumers have no control over the quality, content or price of products.			
2 Businesses try to make as much profit as possible by manufacturing low quality products for sale at high prices.			
3 Economic conditions affect the earnings and the spending of individual consumers.			
4 Most problems experienced by individuals, families, businesses and government are economic in origin.			
5 Consumer behaviour makes a powerful impact on the economy of a nation.			
6 Our economy is controlled by the government.			
7 A major problem in our economy is that wages are not rising as fast as the price of goods.			
8 Unemployment is caused by consumers not spending.			

You can work out similar plans for other subjects by using key words picked out from examination syllabuses and questions: for example, twenty randomly chosen topics from social studies, advertising, alternative lifestyles, choosing, credit, community services, decision making, environment, government, insurance, interdependence, lifestyles, marketing, mass media, needs and wants, pressures, production, resources, supply and demand, trade, values and goals. You can break down each of these topics into paragraphs or sections and suggested activities. Looking at advertising could now produce the following general headings, which you can often put in a question form to provoke a response: What do advertisements do? Who are the major advertisers? What sort of medium do they choose? What controls are they subject to? What is the significance of brand advertising? What is the relationship between information and persuasion? What kinds of techniques do advertisers use? What do people think about advertising?

Alternatively, you can organise your projects around relevant basic skills. Take for example, the theme of owning a car or motorbike. You can develop this in a very active sort of way likely to appeal to students of middle to lower ability.

Example 2: owning a car

Section	Skill	Activity
1 Buying a car	Comparison: reading, listening, analysing	Visiting a motor show, looking at local garages and showrooms, reading newspaper advertisements
	Assessing needs of different individuals	Survey of families and friends on car use
	Graphical skills – form filling, writing cheques, reading, numeracy	Looking at methods of payment
	Personal budgeting	
	Information finding	Using citizens' advice bureaux, *Which?* and manufacturers' associations
	Creativity	Design an advertisement for a car
2 Safety factors	Reading, comprehension, visual comprehension	Using highway code
	Verbal communication	Road safety officer
		Factory visit
	Survey techniques	Seat belt survey
	Numeracy	
3 Insurance	Form filling	Case studies
	Verbal reasoning and role playing	Making statement to police about accident
	Presentation	Making a written statement, with diagrams, about an accident
4 Legal aspects	Numeracy	6 months/1 year tax
	Survey	Comparison of petrol prices
	Interpreting statistics	Imports/oil
	National budgeting	
	Observation and understanding	Conditions of acceptance and garage liability

5	Main- tenance	Numeracy Checking oil, tyre pressures etc. Survey	Case study on repair costs Comparison of motoring organisations and their services
6	Social costs	Using library Map reading Debating skills	Visit to or by an environmental health officer London/rest of country for transport facilities Planning journeys, map comparisons Public versus private transport

Investigation cards

Work cards, assignment cards, the 'busy' cards of the primary school, have the function of providing a specific task, or series of tasks, which students complete in systematic steps. The Department of Commerce at Mynyddbach School in Wales produces a coordinated series of duplicated sheets on topics such as applying for a job, learning how to complain when something goes wrong, money matters in general, savings and investment in particular, budgeting, the fuel famine, wage packets, doorstep selling, safety and so on. Though on a low budget, the Department tries to give its materials an informal eye appeal by using Letraset, and reproducing extracts from newspapers, magazines, and cartoons.

Example 1: cola drinks
1 Find out all you can about cola drinks, their history and how they are made.
   What drug do they usually contain?
   What else is there in them that could be harmful?
2 Fill in the chart on your duplicated sheet that you worked out in group discussion, showing the brands you bought and the shops you got them at. Write down the price paid and the weight of the contents in fluid ounces. Work out which is the best value for money.
   Show on your chart which drinks were bought in cans and which in bottles.
3 Find out whether ingredients are listed on the bottle, whether prices are clearly shown, whether the manufacturer gives his name and address.
4 How easy is it to open each bottle or can? Did your team testing this need a special bottle opener? Did the ring break off any of the cans? Could you turn the caps on the screwtop bottles without too much difficulty?

5   The main advertisement we see is for Coca Cola, which is called 'the real thing'. Find out now – by organising a taste test – if your class can tell Coke from any of the many other cola drinks.
6   How many bottles had returnable deposits? What does this mean in practical terms?
    Do you think it is a good idea to have such deposits? Why? If people don't take their bottles back to the shop, what do you think happens to them? What happens to the tins?
7   Make up a new name for yet another cola drink. Think up a rhyme or jingle that would help you to sell it. Sketch a design for a new bottle, can or totally different kind of container or dispenser. Design an advertisement for a magazine or poster, or make up a television commercial.

Sometimes students themselves can produce work cards to build up a series either for their own group or for a younger year group – the latter providing the satisfaction of superiority. A group of social studies students produced an advertising pack of 50 sheets which could be fairly rapidly worked through. The sheets consisted of pictures cut from magazines, stuck on card (which in retrospect ought to have been plasticised), with questions typed in below. Originally the students used self-adhesive labels for their questions, but if these did not survive being picked at and peeled off they eventually fell off.

Example 2: furniture cream
In the same series as example 3 on page 115, an advertisement for Min furniture cream with the caption 'if Mr Chippendale were alive today, he'd recommend Min' above a picture of a characteristic antique chair leg, highlights students' delight in trying to mislead in the last two questions:

1   Who do you think Mr Chippendale was? What sort of a job did he do?
2   What sort of impression is the writing on the label tied to the chair leg intended to make on you (cursive, elegant handwriting on thick parchment tied with silk ribbon stating 'I would earnestly commend . . .')?
3   What sort of wood is the chair in the picture made of?
4   Who is Min? What is she supposed to do?
5   Where do you think you would be able to find Min? Does the picture tell you?

Example 3: Queen Victoria and the After Eights
1 Who is the old woman in the picture?
2 What time is it (in the advertisement)? Why is this particular time shown?
3 What is this advertisment trying to sell?
4 Usually advertisements have lots of words on them. How many has this one? How does the advertiser try to get his message over to you?

Quizzes, crosswords and word play

Sometimes you need to maintain flagging interest with special inducements which recall, remind and reveal gaps in learning. Work cards can contain a quiz, for example, to be used as a kind of personal test; or quizzes can be used in team competitions within school, against other schools, or even against parents – with a good chance of students winning with a subject like road or home safety. Even the most reluctant students accept quizzes because they are a part of life, appearing prolifically on radio and television as popular entertainment programmes such as

'Mastermind' from which a national champion emerges. Dan and Bill were the leaders of a gang of disturbed, disruptive, extremely low ability fourteen-year-olds who were opposed to any form of learning and authority. But they had a fanatical interest – inspired by Elton John – in football, about which they knew an astonishing amount. Tentatively, their interest in football was diverted into a quiz, with Dan as quizmaster and the rest of the class accepting the discipline of the quiz. Gradually, they were manipulated so that a nonfootball question appeared occasionally, then at frequent intervals, so that in the end general questions dominated. But the quiz was always known as 'the football quiz' and the illusion was kept up successfully until they joyfully left.

Example 1: consumer rights, from Malaysia

How much do you know about your rights, young consumer?

A quiz to test your Consumer Intelligence Quotient (CIQ)

1. Your new pair of suede shoes falls apart after only a month's wear. You return them to the shop, but find that there isn't another pair your size, and you don't like any of the others. The manager says he can only give you a note of credit. Is he right?

≠ Yes   ≠ No

2. You thought that raincoat you bought at the sale was too good to be true at the price it was being offered – it looked alright, apart from a little rip in the seam. But the first time you wore it in the pouring rain, the colour washed away. Well, it was reduced, you think to yourself and you throw it away.

≠ Right   ≠ Wrong

3. When you brought home that piece of meat from the market, there were tiny worms in it which you hadn't noticed when you bought it. Yucks! So you went straight back to the man and demanded a fresh piece.

≠ Smart Move
≠ Not So Smart

4. You go back to the shopping complex with a faulty item but see a notice saying 'Goods Bought Cannot Be Returned. No Money Refunded.' So you go back home, dejected.

≠ Good Thinking
≠ Bad Thinking

5. Boy, were you surprised to receive through the post an expensive book on an esoteric subject. But I didn't order it, you say to yourself. And, while you're wondering what in the world you should do, an invoice arrives asking you to pay up within 14 days! You don't really want the book but you cough up the money anyway because you think you have to.

≠ Right   ≠ Wrong

6. You bought this super handbag for your mother as a birthday present. It turned out to be defective, probably a factory reject. The shop manager refuses to do anything about it, and you threaten to sue him. "You'd be lucky – you'd need a few hundred ringgit for that," he tells you straight in your face.

≠ True   ≠ False

Example 2: safety
1. What colour do you think of when danger is mentioned?
2. What colour do you think of when safety is mentioned?
3. How old do you have to be to buy fireworks? Is it 12, 14, 16, 18, 21?
4. Why do road menders often wear yellow or orange jackets?

5   Sort out these 'safety' words: RSKI, GRANDE, WINGARN, NATIOUC, STAULACY.
6   What is the colour for the earth wire in a three-core flex?
7   Why must you always air dry-cleaned clothes well after you have taken them to the coin-op?
8   If your dog darts out into the road and causes an accident, must you pay for any injuries or damage caused?
9   What is the commonest fatal accident in the home? Is it burns or scalds, poisoning by household products, falls, cuts or electric shocks?
10 Why is lead in paint dangerous, especially to young children?
11 True or false? It is illegal for you to fit your own gas cooker?
12 Draw the symbol you would find on a new electric iron.
13 Why shouldn't you put any sorts of chemical into soft drinks bottles?
14 What is tetanus? Is it:
    - the Latin name for a bad fracture
    - the usually fatal illness caused by the bite of a dog with rabies
    - a blood infection often caused by microbes in the soil?
15 What is asbestos? How is it used in the home? Why must you take special care when using it?

Example 3: a problem solving quiz on safety
What would you do if:

1   The pan you were frying your chips in suddenly caught fire.
2   You found a heap of pills and medicines dumped on a rubbish tip.
3   The small child you were minding swallowed a marble.
4   You had a wasps' nest under the eaves of your house.
5   You saw older boys throwing glass into a children's paddling pool.
6   You saw milk left out on a neighbour's doorstep for a couple of days and the newspaper left sticking out of the letterbox.
7   You saw a friend fall in the canal and you couldn't swim.
8   An elderly relative was coming to stay who couldn't see very well.
9   You wanted to organise a campaign for a pedestrian controlled crossing.
10 Your fingers got stuck together when you were using quick setting superglue.

Not all quizzes need to be devised by teachers. In chapter 3, one of the students in 4b set out to produce a quiz as his contribution

CREDIT

SPENDING AND SAVING

WORKSHEET 17

It is sometimes possible to borrow money for things we would like but for which we do not have the money. This **Worksheet** helps you to think about borrowing (buying on credit) and to bear in mind some of the dangers in doing this.

○ Can you complete this crossword?

ACROSS
4. You own the goods when *all* payments have been made under this method of credit.
5. Amount paid to secure goods.
6. Money borrowed for fixed period with fixed repayments.
7. Extra money paid over and above original loan.
9. When buying on hire purchase, you may not do this during the repayment period.

DOWN
1. Money which you must repay to bank within certain period.
2. What you do when someone lends you money.
3. Used in place of cash or cheque.
4. You may need to ask your bank manager for this, about matters such as taxation, making a will or investment.
8. The percentage you pay in interest.

Spending and Saving Resources Pack Published by **The Life Offices' Association/Associated Scottish Life Offices** Produced by **Peter Rutland Publications**

to the group project: he soon found it was easier to ask the questions than to know the answers. 'What is product liability?' he asked, with only a vague idea of its meaning though a strong conviction of its importance. After discussion – an essential part of a rather surreptitious teaching technique – his group agreed on an answer: 'Your own financial responsibility for any accident you cause.' 'Who is the third party?' he wanted to know – and if there is a third party, who are the first and second parties? Again the answer was discussed and included in his quiz: 'A third party is another person to whom you might cause injury, with you and the insurance company being the first and second parties.'

Crosswords are very time consuming to compose, particularly if you want to produce a pattern. Instead, find a business or commercial example – like the one on page 118 from the Life Offices Association/Associated Scottish Life Offices – which can be duplicated in schools without infringing copyright. If students, like 4b, persist in a desire to create their own, suggest a puzzle with hidden words to find, and supply squared paper. Or suggest jumbled words on a particular theme, such as contract terms, to be sorted out, with the skill lying in the wording of the clue.

Example 1: hidden words connected with safety

caution	danger	warning
risk	BSI	slip
burn	scald	gash
roads	knock	drown
rope	accident	tipping
RoSPA	kick	pond
death	klunck (rather doubtful)	

C	W	X	Y	Z	D	E	A	T	H
D	A	N	G	E	R	R	I	S	K
A	R	U	J	M	O	O	N	L	L
C	N	O	T	P	W	A	Z	I	U
C	I	L	E	I	N	D	T	P	N
I	N	Z	J	R	O	S	P	A	C
D	G	A	S	H	K	N	O	C	K
E	B	U	R	N	Y	U	N	W	I
N	S	C	A	L	D	X	D	F	C
T	I	P	P	I	N	G	Q	U	K

Example 2: jumbled words on contracts

```
      C
   R     A
 N         T       a legally binding agreement between
   C     T         two or more people
      O

      I
 N         N       somebody of either sex who is not yet
                   18
 T         F
      A


      E
 O         F       a proposal made by one party in
                   words or in writing to enter into a
                   legally binding contract with another
 F         R       party


      E
 B         H       this takes place when one of the
                   parties to a contract fails to fulfil one
 C         R       or more terms of the contract
      A
```

Case studies

Case studies should ideally be true – and there is not likely to be a shortage of truth in the examples to be found in the press, particularly local press, in magazines, on the back pages of *Which?*, in correspondence columns and on radio and television, especially in magazine programmes where a personalised story leads on to a general principle.

Take, for example, 'Nationwide's' revelations in July 1983 about 'loan sharks'. This started with investigations into individual cases – the woman who was deprived of her family allowance book completely illegally as security, the mother against whom threats to her home and young children were made if she informed the police or government departments, the couple who had borrowed £50 when they first got married twenty years ago and now owed £2000. The point of the investigation is to alert the public to the fact that they can end up paying 6000% interest, and to urge the Office of Fair Trading to rescind the licences of money lenders known to be unscrupulous, and to be more particular in the first instance when granting one. Correspondence of the air, which is a normal part of regular magazine programmes in presenting public points of view, provides good ancillary educational material. Consequent questions to 'Nationwide's' exposure wanted to know why a government department should need pressure from the mass media before being urged into action, and why people should get into such a mess – wasn't it all their own fault in the first place? There is much for debate and discussion – and personal experience – here.

What, then, is the role of case histories in education? They highlight issues, problems and evils of a general nature, with enough background information about an individual or family as a starting point to provide the basis for solutions and a proposed course of action. In addition to the mass media, organisations such as citizens' advice bureaux, advice agencies, local consumer groups and their federations, and regional branches of nationalised industry consumer councils may be willing to provide help. Obviously, they cannot disclose information given in confidence, but many of the problems and complaints they deal with are similar and can be written up with a fictitious name. Take this example of a complaint received by a gas consumers' council:

Example 1: the new cooker
Mrs Matthews recently bought a new cooker from her local gas showroom. She had never had a cooker like this one before – this one had an oven autotimer. Soon after the cooker was installed in her kitchen, Mrs Matthews and her family decided to go out for a picnic: Mrs Matthews made a casserole, setting the autotimer so that a hot meal would be ready later that evening. And so it was. Mrs Matthews thought it was marvellous to be able to go out and come back to find dinner waiting in the oven.

During the following week she didn't use the oven at all, just cooking breakfasts and dinners on the hob. The following Sunday she made a roast dinner for her family and three friends only to find that the oven wasn't working. She quickly made a salad and opened a can of ham, but she was still very upset the next morning when she reported the fault to the gas board.

The fitter soon came round from the service department and within seconds he had found the fault. 'You haven't turned the timer back from auto to manual', he told her. And he showed her how to do this. A few days later Mrs Matthews was very angry when she received a bill for a call-out charge of £9.

The point for discussion – or even role play – is whether Mrs Matthews was justified in being cross and in refusing to pay.

Or take this example, likewise true, provided by the National Federation of Consumer Groups' Legislation Committee: it could be used within the context of a project on doorstep selling, advertising, contract law or communications:

Example 2: double glazing delivery
Mrs Greenow succumbed to the blandishments of the doorstep salesman of a nationally advertised double glazing firm. She said each time he called in May that the windows would have to be in by September. She signed a contract which did not mention a delivery date, and paid a deposit. She received a rather scruffy and garbled letter dated 29 May confirming the contract, detailing how much she would owe when the windows were installed, giving an estimate of 12–18 weeks and saying they would contact her when they were ready to make arrangements for the installation. She heard nothing more and on 5 October wrote to cancel the contract. On 15 October they replied saying the windows were now ready: they must insist on installing them and receiving the agreed sum. If she refused to have the windows she would owe them nearly as much and they would press for payment.

The point here – again for discussion or role play – is what Mrs Greenow *should* have done, and what she must do now, like finding out how much the firm are asking for if they don't install the windows.

Case histories can be more than just a problem and its solution, an issue and its action; they can be initiated and developed by students themselves rather than imposed by teacher or supervisor, part of a study which can grow and change and even sometimes almost possess the writer. The story of mentally handicapped Norma and elderly Mrs Watson with her Yorkshire reminiscences were part of long studies over the better part of a year, both ending in death, both reluctantly started and sadly terminated. Such studies develop involvement, as the recording of tiny details, perhaps in diary form, builds up into a record not only of progress or deterioration but of concern. Melanie did not like small children very much and she didn't like Asians at all, but she nevertheless consented to go and work in a children's nursery for an afternoon each week – because it was better than being in school – as part of her social studies course.

Example 3: Melanie's diary
'The nurse told me to go and look after Vrinda. I couldn't find her at first – she wouldn't play with the other little children and she was hiding in the Wendy house. So what? Let her stay there for all

I care if she doesn't want to come out. Why should I bother? I did call to her, though, and I peeped through that little door but she hid her face with her hands. Her fingers were brown but her nails were pink like shells. I could see her black eyes looking at me but she wouldn't come out.'

'I went to see the Vrinda again. What's the point? Why didn't her parents give her a proper name that you can pronounce? She was in the Wendy house again. The nurse told me she never said anything at all even though she was three. I called to her feeling silly about that name. She would not come. So I felt in my pocket for a tube of Smarties. All kids like sweets, don't they? I put a red one, a brown one and a pink one in my hand and I said "Sweeties, Vrinda, sweeties". She put out her hand to snatch the sweets and crammed them in her mouth dribbling out red spit. Disgusting I say.'

'It was better this week. I took a book with me. It had pictures of things in it. Vrinda was still in that Wendy house. I called to her. She looked at me through the window and said "Seetie". The nurse looked up. She told me Vrinda had never spoken before. I didn't have any Smarties but the nurse gave me a lump of sugar. Vrinda ate that up dribbling again. I found a tissue and wiped her face. Yerks. "Seetie" she said. "No sweeties" I said "No." She shook her head like me and said "no" too. I started to look at my book. She came out of the house all sticky. "Book" I said. "Book" she said. She turned over the page. I showed her a house, a dog, a tree and other things like that, saying their names. I knew then that she couldn't talk English.'

'Today was great. It was my birthday. When I went to the nursery Vrinda ran up to me and took my hand. "Happy birthday" she said "Present." And she gave me a picture she had painted. There was the Wendy house, there was me drawn pretty big and the nurse even bigger. She had painted herself very small. We all had arms coming straight out of our shoulders and our heads were just stuck on without necks. I like that picture. I shall put it on my wall. I got the book out and sat Vrinda on my knee. She put her arms round my neck. It gave me a sort of warm feeling.'

Reading and comprehension

Once again the press is a significant resource material, both locally and nationally, providing relevant and real situations. But it is wrong to assume that all students have access to newspapers, and those who don't take a paper at home could be embarrassed. Others may not buy the 'right' papers, and your request to 'bring along a paper for tomorrow's lesson' may produce the *Greyhound News*. And there are always those who forget. So, it's a good idea to have a pile of reserve papers and a supply of cuttings, at best filed and recorded on a card index.

Example 1: pesticides awareness
The examples below and on page 125 are articles from the Malaysian press converted into comprehension exercises by the International Organisation of Consumers' Unions.

---

20   SUNDAY ECHO, February 7, 1982

ENVIRONMENT CASEBACK

PESTICIDES: AWARENESS

THERE is a growing world concern that many pesticides being used in the world are dangerous both to farmers and those who consume the food.

This problem is prevalent especially in developing countries of the Third World where there are inadequate controls and sometimes non-existent safety measures on the use of pesticides.

Controversy has also recently built up about the dumping of dangerous pesticides in the developing countries.

Many of these pesticides are banned in Western countries but are exported to the Third World by the same companies which are prohibited from selling their products in their own countries.

Pesticides are being heavily promoted in the Third World to increase the agricultural productivity of these countries.

Our experience with pesticides in Malaysia is a grim warning to other countries of the problems and dangers associated with its use.

SAM's interest in pesticides study began as a result of an increasing number of complaints from workers, estate labourers and farmers of the skin disease, pain and headaches that they suffered at work.

Investigations and a survey among Malaysian farmers ascertained that they were mainly a result of exposure to chemical pesticides the farmers had handled.

Most farms use pesticides as a preventive measure and apply them regularly even though no pest attack may have occurred.

Insecticides are by far the most widely used of pesticides.

Next on the list come herbicides, which act as weed killers in oil palm and rubber estates.

Chemical pesticides are easily obtainable from shops and even sundry stalls.

Malaysian farmers, being mostly ignorant, mainly depend on shopkeepers to recommend them the type of pesticide and advise them on application methods.

At least 72 per cent of farmers fall into this category.

Often, the farmers are not told about the potential dangers to health and the long term draw-backs of pesticides.

Retailers themselves are often not aware of such problems.

Consequently, farmers generally use more pesticides than they should, under the misconception that more chemical pesticides used would mean more pests eradicated.

WOMAN'S DEADLY DRINK

KUALA LUMPUR, Thurs. — Housewife A. Murugamma, 46, died in the General Hospital here today after she accidentally drank a bottle of insecticide in her house at Kuala Selangor yesterday.

She was earlier taken to the Tanjung Karang hospital but when her condition worsened, Mdm Murugamma was referred to the hospital here late last night. She died about 3 a.m.

Her husband, Mr W. Krishnasani, 50, said his wife told him that she was thirsty and drank the insecticide thinking that it was plain water.

He added that his wife complained of dizziness and fainted about 6.30 p.m., 30 minutes after drinking it. — Bernama.

Real issues: real people

1. *How important are pesticides to farming? Can we do without them?*
2. *How great is the need for the introduction of laws to control the application of pesticide, and the amount of pesticide used in food production?*
3. *What are the effects and implications of pesticide poisoning?*
4. *Who is most at risk from pesticides in the food production chain, and how can this risk be eliminated?*
5. *How can reliable, understandable advice on pesticides be made available both to food producers and consumers?*
6. *What sort of publicity is needed to counter general ignorance and lack of care about pesticides? We illustrate this need for awareness by reproducing the sad story of a "Woman's deadly drink".*

See also:
Consumer Lifeline   : Pesticides don't help the hungry.
A Consumer Interpol to blow the whistle.
Leaflets   : Poisoning by pesticide.

Example 2: population planning

"They're poor because they have too many kids" is the commonest of all cliches about world poverty. It is a convenient myth for blaming poverty entirely on the poor.

Until recently it was necessary for poor people to have a large family. Take the case of an ordinary Indian peasant-farmer. His life is plagued by malnutrition and ill-health, with the result that he is too old and weak to work by the time he is fifty (indeed the average person in India dies before his fiftieth birthday). Unless he has sons to support him he will simply die young. But only half his children are likely to be sons and only half of them are likely to survive. Therefore, for very survival, he and his wife need to have a large family.

Now, because of improvements in child health care, more and more people are surviving. But it takes time for an understandably-insecure people to adjust to this trend and compensate for it by having fewer children.

Secondly, the need to have a large family would be dramatically reduced if a man and his wife did not have to die in poverty when they are too old or ill to work — if there was adequate social security, the population increase would automatically slow down. For evidence of this we need only look at the slowing down of population growth in rich countries as these countries have become more affluent.

In other words, large families are more a result of poverty than a cause of it, and in the last analysis prosperity is the best contraceptive.

This increased prosperity for the poor world is not a physical impossibility. It is a fact that the world has enough resources to feed and provide for many times more people than it has at present. Therefore, at the present time, the question of how to achieve a more equal distribution of the world's increasing wealth is more important than the question of how to cut the world's birth rate.

Education for family planning is still an essential part of the fight against under-development. But to blame the poverty of half the world on the population explosion is a mistake which obscures the need for more important changes and stands in the way of their realisation.

"THEY'RE POOR BECAUSE THEY HAVE TOO MANY KIDS"

Real issues: real people

1. This is just one of many misguided assumptions about the causes of poverty and malnutrition. How can these and other misconceptions be corrected?
2. What are the links between family planning and better nutrition and health? How can the message be put over that fewer children can mean better family welfare, and vice versa?
3. What does it mean to say, "Prosperity is the best contraceptive"?
4. Since there are enough resources in the world to feed everybody, how can a fairer distribution of resources be brought about?
5. How can governments be persuaded to invest in social security systems?

See also:
Consumer Lifeline : Malnourishment rises with grain prices.
"The human race is in danger".
Leaflets How to help the hungry.
Hunger in a world of plenty.
Malnutrition.

Photographs are important resource materials for students with low reading skills. A photograph or illustration can help them identify a situation, relate to it, and develop ideas about it, especially when there are questions in simple, logical steps for guidance. You will find useful supplies of illustrations, which include not only photograhs but also cartoons, advertisements, charts and diagrams, in:

- magazines (comics, women's magazines, *Which?*, teenage magazines, fashion journals, mail order catalogues, technical journals, house magazines)

- newspapers (weekly, daily, Sunday – bearing in mind that actual photographs can be available at a relatively low cost)
- government departments (such as the Office of Fair Trading in the United Kingdom, which has a good supply of illustrated leaflets and posters, some specially designed for the teenage market)
- personal photographs (or drawings)

Example 3: housing
Comprehension can be tested in ways other than by merely thinking about responses to traditional questions. In many countries multiple choice questions are increasingly common as a means of encouraging critical thinking. These questions on the squatter problem in Malaysia follow a press article published by the Consumers' Association of Penang. They provide a model for making up similar questions on other social problems:

1. The main cause of the squatter problem is:

    a a general shortage of land in the world
    b the rapid rise in population in the cities due to the migration of people from rural areas where they cannot find jobs
    c the rapid rise in the price of property in the urban areas as compared with the rural areas
    d the existence of vacant houses

2. One possible and effective solution to the squatter problem which could possibly be carried out by the government is:

    a to allow all available property to be sold in the free market
    b to build low cost flats
    c to limit land ownership by the rich
    d to limit land ownership by the rich and make land available to those who need it most

3. The government must involve itself in providing housing for the poor because:

    a if housing is left to the private sector, only those who can afford to pay will get houses
    b the government is likely to make profits from its housing schemes
    c the government is likely to build houses more effectively
    d the private sector is not building enough houses.

    (Answers in the Malaysian context: *b, d, a*).

Sometimes it is not the realism and relevance of the mass media which lead to the creation of the most suitable materials for a given group: your class itself can provide the inspiration for purpose designed stories, inevitably personalised but leading on to general principles. The 'Sally' series featured by the Consumers' Association in *Whichcraft* until 1979 was constructed around incidents and accidents which concerned a real fourth and later fifth year social studies student who had an unbelievable record of mishaps with shoes, dangerous toys for a nephew, pets, leisure activities, old people, customer relationships in a Saturday job, food hygiene . . . and a slug in her sandwich:

Example 4: Sally, the slug and the sandwich

(The cartoon was produced by the New Zealand Consumers' Institute which adapted the story of Sally and David to one about Susan and Daniel.)

Sally and David were coming back from a day on the beach at Clacton. They got quite peckish about six o'clock, but it was Sunday and there were no fish and chip shops open in the towns that they passed through on David's motorbike. At last they found a pleasant little café out in the country where they could sit in the sun and have a quick Coke and a sandwich. David chose a cheese and pickle sandwich, Sally a lettuce and tomato. As Sally sipped her Coke, she noticed something moving on her plate. She looked at it more closely: it was a small grey slug with two horns sticking up, slithering on to the table top now, leaving a slimy trail. She nearly passed out in horror and disgust.

   David went off to get Sally a strong cup of sweet coffee, and to tell the owner of the café what had happened. The owner was most apologetic; she immediately removed the remains of Sally's sandwich and offered to make her another. 'No thanks', said Sally, but she did accept a free dish of strawberries and cream to calm her down.

1. What three things did the owner of the café do? Was there anything else she could have done?
2. Why would the offence have been much more serious (in the eyes of the law, though not in Sally's) if David, for example, had found mouse droppings in his sandwich or mould on his cheese?
3. David did two things. What were they? Was he right?
4. Which Act of Parliament covers food hygiene offences?
   Is it:
   - the Sale of Goods Act 1893
   - the Food and Drugs Act 1955
   - the Trade Descriptions Act 1968
   - the Misrepresentation Act 1967?
5. Do-it-yourself. Is it cheaper? How much would they have spent if they had made their own sandwiches, and bought their cokes from a shop?
6. Though it is dearer to eat out, not all of the extra money is profit for the owner of the café. What sorts of expenses does he/she have?
7. How can you make sure that slugs, snails, greenfly and other livestock don't stick to your lettuce?
8. Sometimes sandwiches have to be kept fresh for some time. How would you keep sandwiches fresh?
9. Make up a recipe for an interesting and nutritious sandwich. Does it make any difference whether you use white or brown bread? What does nutritious mean?

Role playing

Case histories, newspaper and magazine articles, interviews with people, purpose designed stories made up to fit a particular theme are all useful sources of practical learning-by-doing, where your aim is to create situations which your students can then examine more closely to help them cope more effectively and efficiently with similar problems in their own lives. A good role play has certain criteria; it should:

- have a clear purpose which is relevant to the needs of your students
- be carried out in circumstances where it is easy for those taking part to accept the reality of the situation and to identify with the characters

- take place when there aren't the constraints of a 40 minute period – it needs to be free ranging, with time available for group reaction and evaluation
- be organised in a nonauthoritarian way
- be unscripted, and spontaneous, within given guidelines

The advantages of role playing are that it enables students to learn in a memorable way, personalising and permitting them to live out a situation, to deal with conflict (which is an essential ingredient), to work from the particular to the general, and to avoid, at least initially, abstract concepts. Sometimes, of course, it can be necessary for the players to overact in order to make a point. Since a role play should include only the number of students who are *actively* contributing, this means that you are likely to have a large, alert and critical audience: these students are observers, noting which issues are discussed, which decisions made and which reactions take place – but not criticising acting ability. How would they react if they were role players?

After the play, interviewing and deroling involves asking your students questions:

- How did you feel about your role?
- Did your role fit you well?
- Have you been in similar situations before?
- Would you have acted differently in real life?

Deroling is important because it helps students to drop their roles and return to themselves; it also stops them – possibly – from bearing a real life resentment to each other. The audience observes this procedure, but its own special feedback relates to issues that were raised as a result of the action. Role playing demands from you a large amount of preparation time and a great deal of organisational intensity; it is not a technique that all teachers are happy to use, though they generally appreciate its value to students when it is done well. The following two examples outline two real and permanently topical incidents which were duplicated and circulated with notes on characters for guidance. Both were used at a training school for educators, consumers and broadcasters at the Asia/Pacific Institute for Broadcasting Development.

Example 1: cheating at the market
Story
Gaik Sim, on the way home from work at the factory in Petaling Jaya, where she assembles transistor radios, met Pak Gong. They

called in at the local market where they saw a particularly large crowd of people round a man who didn't have a proper stall – just a heap of things on the ground. He was selling panty hose at 50 cents a pair, which Gaik thought was very cheap. So she bought five pairs.

When she and Pak Gong got home, she opened the packets of panty hose to show her mother. She took the first pair out of its sealed cellophane pack, and found that the panty hose had only one leg – and the next pair, and the next. She was so angry that she bundled them all into the rubbish bin. But her father took them out again later to strain his paint through.

Characters

Gaik Sim: You are seventeen and have only just started work at Philips, having had difficulty in finding a job. So you are therefore rather short of money and getting a bargain matters to you. You are known to have a hot temper!

Pak Gong: You are nineteen and have a good deal more sense than Gaik Sim. You get rather cross about the instant decisions she often makes. You think she ought to buy just one pair of panty hose to try out – not five. You feel she would be better off going to a proper shop rather than to a man who doesn't even have a proper stall. You are cross when she throws the hose away.

Salesman: You buy – for almost nothing – rejects from factories. You move on from market to market selling defective hose. You are very charming and persuasive.

Gaik Sim's mother: You appreciate a good relationship with a teenage daughter, but you tell her off for wasting her money on five pairs.

Gaik Sim's father: You tend to shut your ears to 'woman talk', and enjoy getting on with your own hobbies – like decorating and painting. You just want peace and quiet, and everybody to be happy.

Example 2: telephone troubles
Story
Mr and Mrs Cheung have just received their telephone bill. Usually it is quite small because they are not very well off and only use their telephone when it is absolutely necessary. But this time their account is ten times as much as usual. They are desperate because they just don't have the money to pay with – and the

Chinese New Year is just coming up. How can they have spent so much? Have their two teenage children been using the phone? What can they do now? They know their phone will be cut off if they do not pay promptly.

Characters

Mr Cheung: You are a very reliable man who pays all your bills promptly, and you are now very worried, and hurt, by a large bill that you can't possibly pay. You only wanted a telephone in the first place so that you can keep in touch with your elderly parents who live 200 miles away. You wonder if you can ask the telephone company for more time to pay. It never enters your head that the account may be wrong.

Mrs Cheung: You are planning to give your family a happy time at the Chinese New Year, and you know that you won't have any money to spend now. So you get angry and start blaming people. You accuse your children of having used the phone to call their friends. You accuse your husband of not earning enough money to keep your family properly. And finally you accuse the telephone company for being incompetent. You decide to call them at once and give them a piece of your mind.

Ahmei Cheung, Lee Cheung: You are gentle, honest children, twins of thirteen, who never use the phone without asking first. You are upset by your mother's accusations of you and your father. You are sad because you won't be able to celebrate the New Year.

Telephone official: You are the trouble shooter. It is your job to sort out problems and to calm down angry people like Mrs Cheung. You are very patient and try hard to get accurate details from her. You tell her – at last – that you think there is a mistake in the account.

Both these examples were taped, and since the participants knew that this was happening they included sound effects to emphasise their points – easier to achieve because they had received their background papers the night before. Given the opportunity, role plays can be videoed; this, though destroying the simultaneous spontaneity of immediate discussion, has the advantage of enabling debate to be delayed until time is available and of providing a real life dramatisation which you can refer to other groups. Students in the Education Department of Goldsmiths' College, London University did a role play based on one of the stories about Sally. There was no script, the words being transcribed only after the video tape had been made:

Example 3: Sally and the shoes
(Credit over shot of two feet – one a girl's, one a boy's)
(Pull back to four feet in shot)
(Mixed laughter)

Sally:	Oh, David!
David:	No, I'm telling you – it really happened! (Sally laughs. Pause)
David:	Um, by the way . . . have you heard Rod Stewart's latest?
Sally:	Yeah – it's great.
David:	Well, Rod Stewart's singing at the Odeon on Saturday – fancy going?
Sally:	I don't *think* I'm doing anything this Saturday.
David:	Well, you are now, Sally, meet you outside – half past seven on the dot. See you there.
Sally:	Yeah, see you then. (David's feet exit) (Camera tilts up to Sally's face slowly as she says).
Sally:	I think I'll wear that blue dress – but I'll have to buy some shoes – I know, I can get them after work on Saturday. (Mix through to row of chairs – shop. Assistant is sitting down, bored. Slam of door – in rushes Sally)
Assistant:	Yes?
Sally:	Have you got those blue sandals with the high heels in the window in size 5?
Assistant:	Do you mean the ones reduced to nine ninety-nine?
Sally:	Oh, I'm not sure . . . . (Assistant leaves shot – as if in window. Sally looks to her)
Sally:	Yeah, those there – to the left, to the left. (Assistant returns)
Assistant:	You're lucky – we have got these in your size. I'll just get a pair. (Assistant leaves shot – Sally sits in chair,

	impatiently counting out money etc. Assistant returns with shoes, bends down to try them on Sally's feet)
Sally:	No, I haven't got time to try them on – they'll be okay. Here's the money.
	(Assistant takes money, stands – camera follows rise of assistant and films her writing out receipt and taking penny change out of her pocket)
	(Assistant turns back to Sally)
Assistant:	Here you are, d. . . . .
	(Camera follows assistant's glance to *empty* chair – door slams off screen)
	(Camera remains on chair – with assistant's hand (and receipt and penny) in shot)
	(Mix through to hairdressing salon – Mary (Sally's friend) is sitting in chair having hair done by Sally)
Mary:	That same day? I don't believe it.
	(Camera pulls back to include Sally)
Sally:	Honest. I bought them at five, and by eight o'clock the left heel had snapped right off. I mean, I wouldn't have minded so much if we'd been dancing a lot, but we'd only just arrived.
Mary:	So what did you do?
Sally:	Ooh! and David was that mad because we couldn't dance all night – I wasn't going to dance on that floor in my bare feet – so we just sat there like a couple of old dears all night.
	(Pause – camera closes in on Sally alone)
Sally:	Ooh, just wait till I get in that shop tonight!
	(Mix to face of shop assistant)
	(Mix to shop assistant's face – looking annoyed, as being told off by manager)
(Voiceover)	
Manager:	It's really not good enough, Miss Robinson, I asked you to complete that stock list two weeks ago – have you started?
Assistant:	Look, there's only me here – and we've been very busy recently.
	(Cut to shot of manager over girl's shoulder)
Manager:	Busy? Busy? The takings don't show that. I want that list, Miss Robinson, by nine thirty tomorrow morning, otherwise . . . . (Door slams open – they turn – cut to Sally looking annoyed, holding shoes in box)

(Voiceover)
Manager: Customer, Miss Robinson.
Sally: Hello – I bought these shoes here last Saturday for ten pounds and the first time I wore them, the heel snapped right off – look.
(Sally goes to pull out shoe, but before broken shoe is revealed – cut to assistant)
Assistant: Where's your receipt?
(Voiceover)
Sally: Receipt?
Assistant: If you bought them here, you'd have been given a receipt. (Assistant moves towards Sally)
Assistant: Isn't it in the box?
(Sally looks in the box)
Sally: No, there's no receipt here – you never gave me a receipt.
Assistant: We don't exchange goods or refund money without a receipt. Sorry.
(Assistant goes to walk away – Sally calls her back)
Sally: But they cost me ten pounds – that's five Saturday's work – and they broke after three hours. They're no good to anybody like this. What am I going to do?
Assistant: You should have thought of that last Saturday and waited for your receipt. Sorry, dear.
(Assistant walks off)
(Cut to Sally's face, camera tilts down to her feet and rubbish bin. Shoes drop in bin in box. Sally's feet leave screen – camera pass to shoes in box in bin. Door slams – fade and music)

Script writing

Scripts – readymade – can be incorporated into assignment cards on a specific project. It is part of the American Consumers' Union's normal practice in its teaching materials to provide a script which has to be read, interpreted and taped by the student – and sometimes, as the example used in chapter 5 shows, used in real circumstances.

Much more difficult and much more satisfying is the actual creation of a script suitable for taping or radio use. Listening to current programmes, observing them carefully, can give a great deal of insight into the opportunities and ingenuity of cheaply produced local radio programmes. In the example that follows, knives, forks and spoons are jangled together to simulate the surgical instruments in a busy hospital.

A magazine programme gives a great deal of scope and it allows different groups to provide an input coordinated by a director using music and link words. The following example is the transcript of a programme devised in Malaysia as a training exercise, again for educators, consumers and broadcasters, with serious subjects dealt with casually but emphatically.

Announcer: The time is ten o'clock. From Radio CX1, here's your consumer friend.
(Music: signature tune)

Nanette: Good morning, folks. This is your regular consumer friend, Nanette, ready to join you with your morning coffee. Today we have invited DJ Dave to chat with us about your consumer problems. Hi Dave! Welcome to the show.

Dave: Hello.
Frankly, I'm feeling a bit awkward here – I've never discussed consumer problems before, you know.

Nanette: Oh, no problem – I'm sure you're familiar with the use of . . . let's say . . . crash helmets.

Dave: Oh ya! I just bought a 250 cc Suz . . . .

Nanette: Uh-Uh! no commercials on this programme. Anyway, let's rattle off the rest of the consumer problems that we've got in store for our friends this morning.
Breastfeeding . . . .

Dave: Hey! You know, I was breastfed for a whole year!

Nanette: Did you enjoy it?

Dave: Sure, I enjoyed it . . . .
(Both laugh)

Nanette: Seriously now Dave, we're quite fortunate to get an exclusive interview with Dr Sam Abraham . . . .

Dave: Oh, he's the well known paediatrician.

Nanette: Uh-huh, and with Azizah Hamid from the nursing profession on breastfeeding. We also have something interesting on foods in dented cans, pollution in general and a whole lot more.

Dave: It certainly sounds like a polluted morning.

Nanette: That's Dave's polluted mind working. Remember, we have DJ Dave with us this morning. So stick around folks.
(Music)

135

Nanette:	Dave, you've met Amelia. Yeh, our field interviewer, right?
Dave:	Ya, she interviewed me the other day on a pop show.
Nanette:	In that case you haven't heard the serious side of Amelia. Let's hear her now from the maternity ward of the University Hospital. Listen closely, Dave – it's your favourite subject . . . breastfeeding.
Amelia:	Good morning. I have with me Azizah Hamid, one of the staff nurses at the maternity ward here. Cik Azizah, what is the position of this hospital regarding breastfeeding?
Azizah:	We encourage mothers to breastfeed for at least the first six months.
Amelia:	I understand there have been cases of sales girls dressed up as nurses selling milk powder. What have you to say about that?
Azizah:	We are definitely against such unethical practices. This is especially serious when these so-called nurses approach uneducated, low income mothers who may not be able to afford it and still buy milk powder. What the sales girls do not tell the mothers is how much powder to use to how many ounces of water, and how to keep the bottles clean. When the bottles are not properly sterilised, the babies fall ill, develop diarrhoea, which may lead to more serious complications.
Amelia:	Why don't modern mothers breastfeed?
Azizah:	Ironically, it's mostly for beauty reasons. They do not realise that the uterus contracts when you breastfeed – and this hastens the slimming process. You might even say breastfeeding is beautifying!
	(Music)
	(Sound effects: knives, forks and spoons)
Amelia:	At the children's ward of the same hospital, where you can hear the sounds of surgical instruments being sterilised in the background, I am right now with Dr Sam Abraham, a firm believer in breastfeeding.
Dr Abraham:	We have a very important international paediatrics congress coming up in February. The most important issue tabled is breastfeeding. I

|||||| would like to stress that the Malaysian Paediatric Society is presenting a position paper stating that local manufacturers and distributors of milk powder refrain from pushing the use of powder in hospitals and government owned institutions.

Amelia: Thank you, Doctor. This is Amelia from the University Hospital handing you back to Nanette and Dave in our studios.

Nanette: Thank you, Amelia. Dave, you're from Penang, right?

Dave: No, I'm from Perak.

Nanette: Oh, that's right – well, never mind, they sound the same.

Dave: You really are a nut.

Nanette: Anyway, Amelia's also been to Juru, a fishing village in Penang that was literally dying, slowly losing its sole means of livelihood beause of pollution. Let's hear from Amelia who flew to Penang last Sunday.

(Tape: three seconds, sound effects of motor boat)

Amelia: I hope you can hear me above the noise of the motor boat. Well. I have just asked Encik Samad here, he's one of the councillors of Juru who is himself a fisherman, what happens to the river when waste matter is pumped from the factories.

(There then follows a tape in Bahasa Malaysia about the polluted village, and this section ends with Dave reciting a poem)

Dave: We blind mice
We blind mice
See what we've done
See what we've done
We all ran after progress's wife
Who cut off our heads with development's knife
Have you ever seen such fools in your life
As we blind mice?

All the skills and strategies developed in this chapter show a very broad interpretation of the word 'project', in the conviction that any subject, even within existing constraints, can become active, original, even committed in its approach. Traditionally, teachers accept that there are four basic teaching techniques, certainly for lower level exam courses:

- teacher explanation
- questions and answers
- discussion
- worksheets and exercises

And these techniques, according to a survey carried out in 1980 among 1454 economics and commerce students by the Computer Centre at Hatfield Polytechnic, take up over 80 per cent of all teaching time. The remaining 20 per cent goes on field studies, programmed learning, games and simulation, television and films – and on projects.

But a project is not something to be separated off in this way from the generality of learning, for it transcends these four traditional classifications. It incorporates, for example, 'teacher explanation' in briefing sessions for students; it includes discussion, the use – and even creation – of worksheets, questioning and answering, though putting no restriction on who asks and who answers. A project is an essentially personalised 'compound' of traditional and experimental approaches with an infinitely variable input – and the expectation of an equally variable but tangible output.

5 Presenting the results of a project

Projectors in action

Gill and June, Brenda, Melanie and Lynne wrote and produced a little book called *Souvenir*. They had never written a book before, and they certainly hadn't been very keen on starting. But this was a book with a useful difference: it consisted of all kinds of information for the foreign exchange visitors who came to their school every summer from St Ismier in France.

Though none of the five girls had ever been abroad herself, they were aware of different currencies and realised that their visitors' first need would be to change money. With the written consent of their parents, they went off to find out where the banks were, what times they opened ('Do you know, Miss, they are shut on Saturdays?'), what sort of identity check was needed, what other agencies dealt in currency exchange, and who gave the best rate. Did it cost anything to change money, and what happened if you had anything left over when you went back home? All this formed the basis of chapter 1; they wrote it up in longhand, found some amusing cartoons they could 'borrow', and typed it out in commerce. They felt much more confident now, and ready to face chapter 2.

After some argument they decided that a foreign visitor would have been given orders to write home straight away 'because parents always worry until they have heard that you have arrived safely'. 'If you ask nicely your new family will probably provide you with your first stamp', but after that they could expect to be on their own. The girls mapped out positions of post offices, learning the difference between a Crown post office and a sub post office; they found out the rates for cards and letters to Europe; they gave the best sources of local post cards; they pointed out that post boxes 'will be red, not yellow or blue as they are in France'. It was in this section that they made a mistake. Overconfident, they did not continue to check each other's findings and they got the postal rates wrong; nor did they find this out until their book was nearly ready for distribution – so they had

WELCOME!

Cecile Redmond, Florence Jegoudez, Bérénice Jacobé, Agnès Garat, Isabelle Lachaux, Patrick Ligeon, Christine Boinnard, Florence Chevallier, Eric Collin, Catherine Noiray, Nadine Relave, Claire Saurel, Martine Verdier, Marie-Dominique Agay, Serge Bailleul, Christine Bergerat, Jacques Demians, Eric Thomas, Jean Luc Rizzo, Thierry Dardalhan, Sylvain Admirat, Alexis Zaslavoglou, Thierry Avenier, Eric Munoz, Jacques Michelot, Olivier Champion, Frederic Geindre, Bernard Jay

vous voici en vacances...

the bother of sticking in erratum slips. 'What's "erratum", Miss?' They were much more careful when they came to chapter 3, which – logically – dealt with finding telephones in public places, how to dial a foreign country, how to deal with home sickness: 'If you are desperate to hear a French voice, you can telephone 01 246 8043 and you will get an account in French of the main events of the day in and around London.' And: 'Remember it is cheaper to make a call in England during the evening. Ring Mum then and not during the day.'

They then proceeded with their major section on 'what to buy and where to get it', looking at the market, small shops, chain stores, department stores, finding out variations in shop opening hours. Their main aim was to be able to suggest value-for-money souvenirs for their visitors to take home (they rather liked a melamine ash tray complete with St George and the dragon), and presents for specific members of their families. They compiled tables of equivalent weights and measures for reference when choosing. They thought tea or teabags would be a good present for Grandma, T shirts, tights, socks or model kits for brothers and sisters, marmalade or mincemeat for Mum ('It's a mixture of things like currants, raisins, suet, apple and candied peel that we put in pies at Christmas time'), a small whole English cheese, like Wensleydale, for Dad, and an enamel or earthenware teapot for Grandad ('since they don't go in for proper teapots much in France'). They commended British posters and records as good general buys.

Saletime

Soldes   **Sales**

You have arrived at a very fortunate time of the year if you want to save money: at this time of the year many shops are holding their *summer sales* at which there can be fantastic bargains if you look carefully. In London people sometimes go quite mad, queuing all night for a fur coat or a bedroom suite. In Hemel Hempstead you won't see this kind of madness, though in Watford a departmental store called Clements always ends its three weeks of sale time with what is called Blue Cross Day: people do queue here from the early hours of the morning for something which is important to them, since the final price is now half the sale price. We don't advise you to go in at dawn, but rather about nine o'clock when the long, winding queue will have disappeared. There will still be plenty of bargains left.

    According to our fairly recent laws, reductions in price on sale goods have to be real, so you can now see what you are saving by comparing the original price with the sale price. Special purchases and ends of manufacturer's ranges can be very good buys, but if you are buying goods marked 'seconds', these will have some defect somewhere. Look carefully. Look even more carefully at goods marked 'substandard'. These may have a big fault, such as a pair of tights only having one leg!

Things to look out for
Clothes, especially summer clothes, since this is now the end of the summer shopping season; socks, shoes and tights; pottery, where you may find seconds of famous names like Wedgwood; glassware, household linens, stationery, jewellery.

The girls then investigated getting around and about by public transport, with times, prices and distances, and they provided a checklist of things to fill in: have you seen . . . a zoo, a cathedral, a cricket match, a safari park? They thought people in their age group liked filling in details, so they also added a checklist for food: have you tasted . . . fish and chips, jelly, trifle, sausages and mash, shepherd's pie?

    And they ended with their own list of 'useful things to know about the British', which they produced after much deliberation. This included:

- milk is brought to the house by the milkman every day, in *pints*
- people are usually very orderly and queue for things like buses
- they eat with a knife in their right hand and a fork in their left
- they love listening to weather forecasts on the radio or TV
- they are always eating sweets
- they stand on the right going down escalators in the Underground

The girls gradually built up a logical programme of procedure. They discussed what they were going to do, decided on the work sharing, carried out their research, got their findings checked by another member of the group, typed it all out in rough, planned headings with Letraset and added illustrations, rearranged it all and retyped it ready to take off to the teachers' centre where they were allowed to learn about offset litho. Duplication would have been satisfactory, but there would have been more of a problem with stencil cuttings and the provision of illustrations and headings.

Everything was ready by the time the foreign visitors arrived. They themselves were not part of the exchange, and at first had not been at all keen on doing anything for anybody from over the Channel. But they glowed with pride at the reception of their book. After all, no one else in the school had actually written a book for people to use. And they took a party of French girls shopping to buy St George and the dragon.

What sort of presentation?

This introductory example shows a project where final use clearly determines method of presentation. The girls knew from their rather reluctant beginning that, in their case, they would need to produce some sort of publication 'so as those foreigners can carry it round with them'. But the end product – and it is vital that there should be some sort of outcome to motivate, encourage and even discipline students – can appear in any appropriate form. Obviously, when students are carrying out a project for a particular exam, or even as a competition entry, there are certain rules and conventions which affect presentation. But even here there can be alternative versions: with economy of effort in mind, the girls rewrote *Souvenir* as a CSE social studies project on tourism, though admittedly it would be more usual for the exam project to come first and then be adapted to suit other needs. A presentation, then, can range from a public exhibition on food and

The cover illustration for *Souvenir*, featuring the dragon, an English dog rose and a French cockerel

nutrition in Georgetown or Jakarta, Bangkok or Bangalore, to audio/video montages on energy consumption in Alsace or Adelaide, to actual product development of reclining wheelchairs or water filtration plant in the United Kingdom. Projects can incorporate any appropriate method of communication: leaflets, guides, booklets, flip charts, murals and wall charts, mobiles, posters, photographs and slides, recordings, drama and role play, debates and discussions, and increasingly computer software. But the major emphasis in this chapter will be on the presentation of findings in report form.

A written or an oral report?

It's an important asset to be able to talk in front of an audience, to put forward a logical and convincing case with confidence, to stand up to searching and sometimes aggressive questioning, to face unresponsive passivity and a complete lack of interest. This is an important life skill, not only at work, but also at home in the context of claiming benefits, facing tribunals, appealing against income tax assessments, appearing in the county court, and so on. Moreover, there is a growing number of external exams, even at a lower level, which include face-to-face interviews with an examiner or require the submission of a taped interview. Confidence and self-assurance are difficult skills to teach to those who haven't got them, but order, organisation and a set of familiar rules can help:

- Students must all talk, improvise, from the scant security of short paragraph headings – they mustn't read out an essay they have prepared in advance.
- They must keep to a set time limit – even experienced adults find they have a very vague concept of time when asked to talk for five minutes, and enormous optimism about the number of points they can make with any conviction.
- They may have the support of some visual aid – a poster, a flip chart, a set of overhead projector transparencies or slides can give reassurance as well as provide a framework.
- They must be able to have full confidence in their teacher, not only to maintain law and order but to act as a 'prompt' and prevent someone from losing face. 'That's fine so far. So what did you do next?' is often enough to help a stumbling student.
- The rest of the class must have a positive and not a passive role, taking notes, using structure patterns to reveal the logic and completeness of the presentation, writing summaries, asking questions, evaluating, thinking about the next steps to take.
- Students should be given normal adult courtesies, be properly introduced at the beginning (another student can be delegated to do this) and thanked at the end.

Though there is no doubt about the importance of an oral report, the emphasis is on written reports, for a variety of reasons. Firstly, many exam boards require them as tangible proof of knowledge and skills, and examiners can mark written materials at their own convenience. Secondly, they are semi-permanent and can be reproduced relatively easily. Thirdly, the ability to write a structured report can be essential both at home and at work, in social activities and in voluntary service. Written and oral project reports have, nevertheless, certain things in common; both require:

- an indication of the original aim of the project and who it is intended for. A few words may be needed about changes which have taken place in the course of work: for example, a local survey on the provision of public lavatories for the disabled came to nothing because there weren't any, but a nonresult turned into a successful campaign for making all public places easier to get into

- an outline of methods used to carry out the project, together with the results of observations, inquiries and investigations, together with conclusions and reflections
- an emphasis on verification at all stages, checking facts, figures, sources, and listing those that are referred to

Writing a report

Planning, collecting and organising information is in chapter 3, and a variety of strategies for investigation in chapter 4. Students are now at a stage when they can think about writing up the results of their findings, which appear in five main sections or stages:

- title and contents
- introduction
- main section
- conclusion
- appendixes and references

But students don't necessarily have to write these sections in the order in which they finally appear – in fact, it is often as well to write the introduction last at the same time as the conclusion, when they have carried out their investigations.

Title

This is likely to be the first thing that attracts the reader. Its function is to provide a summary, in three or four words, of the point of the project – *Saving your money*, *Danger in the home* and *Public transport services* give an immediate idea of what to expect. But generic titles like these need a subtitle to modify their content if the subject is too large or too vague, and to give further explanation. So, *Saving your money* becomes more precise and defined by the addition of the subtitle 'An appraisal of the methods used by young people' or, more aggressively, 'Are building societies and banks the best bet for young people?' The other two subjects become *Danger in the home*: 'An investigation into the causes and prevention of accidents to old people in North Hertfordshire'; and *Public transport services*: 'An evaluation of facilities available in Adelaide'.

Alternatively, given freedom of choice, titles can intriguingly start with the particular and move towards the general: *Looking after Lucy*: 'A study in child care based on experience at Bennetts End Day Nursery'; or *Bill and his old banger*: 'The problems young people face when buying their first car or motorbike'. Gill, June, Brenda, Melanie and Lynne did not use any of this guidance, however, but came up with a simple one word title – *Souvenir* – for their tourist guide. It is an excellent title, playing on the difference in meaning of the word in English and French, fitting the purpose for which the girls intended it.

Contents

The contents page, sometimes wrongly referred to by students as the index, provides a quick insight into the scope of the project. Sadly, a project may stand or fall by its indicators; its chapter or paragraph headings. These should be informative, attractive and designed to arouse both interest and curiosity. Questions are often useful as headings: there is more impact in 'How many people were killed on the roads?' than in 'Statistics concerning the number of deaths on the roads'.

Project reports usually start off with a contents page, but it is acceptable to put a short introduction first instead. The steps to follow are:

- Decide on the main headings, which your students may well like to describe as chapters, since there is a certain appeal in following an accepted adult and professional procedure.
- Decide on the subheadings for each chapter.
- Work out a suitable numbering scheme. Chapter headings could have Roman numerals, for example, and the subheadings Arabic, providing that students know the difference between the two. Any further divisions of the subheadings could be identified by italic letters. Or students could take a look at the system frequently used in Open University publications where each chapter has an Arabic number followed by a paragraph or subheading number. For example, 2.4 would be the fourth paragraph in the second chapter.
- Make a list of illustrations so that these can be referred to quickly – p 26 Fig 4 – and decide whether these are to appear separately or be incorporated into the main contents page.
- Number the pages in the top right hand corner, pencilling them in until the final order is certain.
- Decide whether the introduction is to be included in the numbering system or left to stand on its own.
- Add page numbers, well aligned, to the list of chapter and subheadings on the contents page. Check that these numbers fit those in the body of the report.

Introduction

Since the introduction is the first thing to be read, the opening lines have special significance. Examiners and subject teachers *have* to read project reports, but that doesn't stop them from suffering from boredom; other people don't have to read something that doesn't attract and retain their interest. 'How do I start, Miss?' is the question frequently asked. The answer is that in reading or discussion someone may have said or done something which sums up the whole project: 4b's study on safety, in chapter 3, provided the memorable quotation 'safety's boring, accidents is interesting' as an ideal opening sentence. Those who have worked with children, hospital patients or old people in the course of their project generally find some appropriate, often funny, comment they can quote. Or incidents featured in newspapers can link up with a project under way. A look at the ways in which journalists start and end articles can also give practical guidance to students, as long as they realise that journalists' copy can be cut short by editors.

In addition to the drama and dynamism of the opening sentence (which is a matter of personal taste and practical convention), the introduction has a series of important and specific functions:

- to point to the *purpose* of the report and show how far it has been possible to achieve it
- to provide any necessary definitions. Even obvious things need to be defined, and it is still more important where ambiguity is possible: for example, *Foreign aid and development*: 'A study of north/south relationships'. Does 'development' mean the extension of foreign aid, or does it mean the relationship between aid and progress in developing countries?
- to give relevant background information
- to summarise the conclusions of the project (it is this point which shows students why they can't normally write their introduction first)
- to provide where appropriate a list of recommendations. If these turn out to be very compelling, then they can be set apart on a new page to be focused on immediately after the introduction
- to give a general view of the subject without the clutter of detail which detracts from the main thrust of the argument; and at the same time to pick out occasional points worthy of special emphasis
- to acknowledge the help given by particular individuals and organisations; if this is a long list, or if special diplomacy is called for, then acknowledgments can go on a separate page.

Main section: organisation, rejection and verification

For this stage there is likely to be a mixed collection, sometimes dauntingly large, assembled from notes, books, newspaper cuttings, people interviewed and investigations carried out. All this must be sorted and presented so that people can understand it. The final users of the project and their special needs must never be forgotten – as Melanie insisted, 'We must make the English easy so as they can understand.' If readers are kept in mind as information piles up, then *organisation* will be simpler. But invariably there will be more facts and ideas than students can use, and it is very painful for them to have to throw out something laboriously acquired over a long time. There is a strong instinct to collect, retain – and relate – everything! They need strict self-discipline to face up to the reality of *rejection*. The questions they should ask themselves about the information they have collected are:

- Has this really got anything to do with the part of the subject I have chosen?
- Is all my information absolutely correct?
- Is my subject too big and unwieldy? If so, which part shall I choose to concentrate on?

It is also essential to behave responsibly over *verification*. It is easy – but not honest – to trust to memory, setting down half recalled facts or giving doubtful figures the stamp of certainty. It is easy to supply inadequate or incomplete information, particularly about sources which a reader may want to follow up. And everyone, however skilled, makes mistakes in adding up, placing a decimal point, spelling a name, interpreting even their own handwriting. Melanie made a mistake in timing: between investigating postal rates to France and 'going to press', there was a price increase which she did not know about, not having checked in the final stages. Her group, which reproached her more than enough, consequently had to type out and stick in 100 correction slips, which they found very boring. *Which?* magazine employs special staff called verifiers who at every stage check reports they have not been involved in writing. Even so, mistakes and consequent

CORRECTION

Getting legal advice, *Which?*, October 1982
On page 590, we said that law centres specialise in divorce (among other things). In fact they do not generally deal with divorce, so although they may give preliminary advice about this, they will almost always refer those seeking help to a solicitor in private practice at an early stage.
    On page 591 we said that the cost of having a legal bill taxed is five per cent of the disputed bill, unless you get the bill reduced by a fifth or more. This is true, but if you *don't* get the bill reduced by this much, you will also have to pay the other side's costs of dealing with the taxation. We also said, on page 591, that the *fixed fee scheme* for preliminary advice from a solicitor does not exist in N Ireland. In fact it does operate there, too.
    We are sorry about these mistakes.

apologies still appear in the magazine. But students are not going to have an independent verifier, and even with the best of intentions can easily slip into a passive acceptance of their own writing as they are overwhelmed by the demands and boredom of checking – and not just checking once but at several stages. If you tell them why verification is important, they may take more care: the report loses credibility, and any recommendations their force, if the reader, who may well be an examiner, detects errors of fact. Inaccuracy and misinformation can be unfair to a person misquoted; wrong figures can be commercially, economically, socially and politically unjust and misleading; and even schools are not exempt from the law of libel.

Organisation, *rejection* and *verification* will cut down the amount of information which should now be allocated to its specific chapters, sections or subgroups. Students can often treat these as separate units, each one with its own miniplan dealing with particular aims, their implementation and development.

Checklist for students

- consider the logical order in which to present these separate units, especially if members of a group have each been working on a different aspect. It is not a case of fighting for 'mine first'
- arrange the material in each unit so that the reader can follow it step by step
- work out headings so that they entice and inform
- introduce illustrations and diagrams where these are likely to add impact and explanation, or indeed be more informative than words; consider where they are to be mentioned in the text using a systematic reference scheme
- pick out possible conclusions and recommendations for promotion
- take out for inclusion in an appendix those bits where detail distracts the reader from major issues. A questionnaire, for example, could go in an appendix, unless the need for it is got rid of altogether by using the questions as paragraph headings in the text
- make a list of sources of information that have been used so that these can appear as bibliography in an appendix. Similarly, note down any technical or specialised terms that need to be explained in a glossary together with abbreviations. Decide if an index would be useful to the reader

Conclusion

There won't be anything new in the conclusion. Its function, depending on what appears in the introduction, is to summarise briefly and draw together ideas, arguments and the results of investigations, and to put forward any recommendations. Some students find controlled and organised stopping almost as difficult as starting. Again a quotation can be useful, or a final paragraph called 'The future?' or 'What next?' outlining the events that are likely to follow from those described in the report.

Appendixes and references

It's not always necessary to have a large collection of appendixes, or indeed any at all. But they can be useful when more detailed explanations need to be provided for specialists; here they don't obscure the line of thought, they can be read at leisure and they can come in any shape or size. Bibliography fits into a special appendix as part of the honest approach of acknowledging services rendered. A project is not 'looking things up in lots of different books and copying them down': an examiner is a good detective, may know the source and will certainly recognise a difference in style. Direct quotations from books or papers should be numbered in sequence in the text, with full information given at the foot of each page as well as in an appendix. This is easier for students than to put all sources quoted at the end of each chapter, or indeed at the end of the report. You need to remind them that they must give the page number (and that the abbreviation for the plural of pages is pp); likewise, they needn't mention a title more than once – they can use *op cit*, the Latin for 'work already quoted'. But when a title is given in full it must be done properly in a recognised style, eg Fulani D, *The Price of Liberty*, Hodder & Stoughton, 1981.

Alternatives to words

The newspaper photograph on page 151 shows more effectively and concisely than any written description the dangers small children encounter in the kitchen. But such a picture still cannot stand completely on its own: it needs possibly a caption or heading and certainly a short explanation of the issue at stake. John, in 4b's safety project in chapter 3, called the picture 'casualty in the kitchen' and gave details and acknowledgements underneath: 'Photo by *Eastern Evening News*, Norwich, showing a small child with her hands burnt because the outside temperature of the oven door was too hot.'

It is not just photographs which enliven, activate and even abbreviate a project, but a whole range of illustrations, of charts, maps, tables, graphs and diagrams. The following checklist applies to any kind of illustration:

- try to refer to it briefly in the text
- work out a simple reference system: Fig 1, 2, 3 and so on

(remembering that 'Fig' has been known to be misunderstood) if the illustrations are varied, and Table 1, 2, 3 if the emphasis is on numbers
- label component parts of a diagram neatly and clearly, from the same side where possible
- put the illustration as close as possible to the reference in the text
- reserve a general summary illustration for the frontispiece, or even for the cover
- write short captions where necessary
- give acknowledgments if the illustration does not belong to you – copyright clearance would also be necessary if the project were for public use. Don't cheat or steal: though the girls

writing *Souvenir* could never understand what was wrong in cutting out and using small cartoons – 'but they'll never find out, Miss. What's the harm?'

Pictures

Carefully chosen pictures (like the photo of the child and the cooker), drawings and diagrams can highlight a situation, show how things work, or even introduce a subject. Such illustrations fall into two categories. Firstly, there are those which students actually produce themselves, choosing the specific aspect of the subject they want to emphasise. Photographs are particularly good at providing proof and substantiation of their case. Secondly, there are those which students cut out of magazines and newspapers, photocopy or – in the case of diagrams – redraw themselves. Illustrations of both kinds are a particular asset to less able or less literate students, who can produce a well researched project consisting almost entirely of pictures on a suitably visual subject such as advertising, packaging, labelling, food, clothes or housing. A child care project appears as a well selected, well headed, logically arranged photograph album which should not be underrated just because it looks comparatively easy to produce. But there are warnings about using photographs: a member of the same year group wanted to use the same technique for his study of a mental hospital and could not understand why he was not allowed to take pictures freely. 'It's not fair – and they like having their pictures took.' There are firm rules in state institutions and these must be stuck to.

The examples on pages 153 to 156 show the power of illustrations to supplement or replace words:

Example 1: from South Korea
This forms part of a multimedia project on children's toys and is drawn specifically to show a 'son baby's' preference for war toys.

Example 2: from Sri Lanka
This is a preliminary sketch for a project on water and sanitation, showing how lake water used for drinking, bathing and washing clothes is polluted by the drainage from communal latrines built in the midst of two groups of houses.

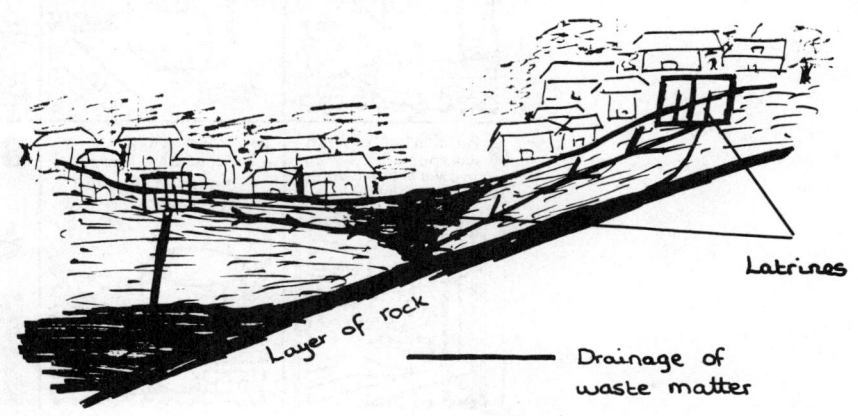

Example 3: aerosol
This provides the answer to a fifteen-year-old's problem in a packaging project – how does an aerosol work? Page after page of long winded yet incomplete descriptions were thrown out in anger before she found a simple diagram in *Which?* that explained how an aerosol worked.

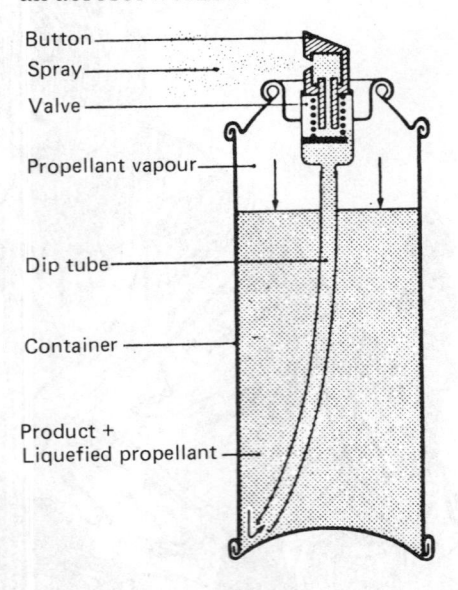

Example 4: yoghurt
This shows how instructions can be reinforced by pictures, or even by cartoons using 'bubbles' and preferably lower case letters for commentaries and comments.

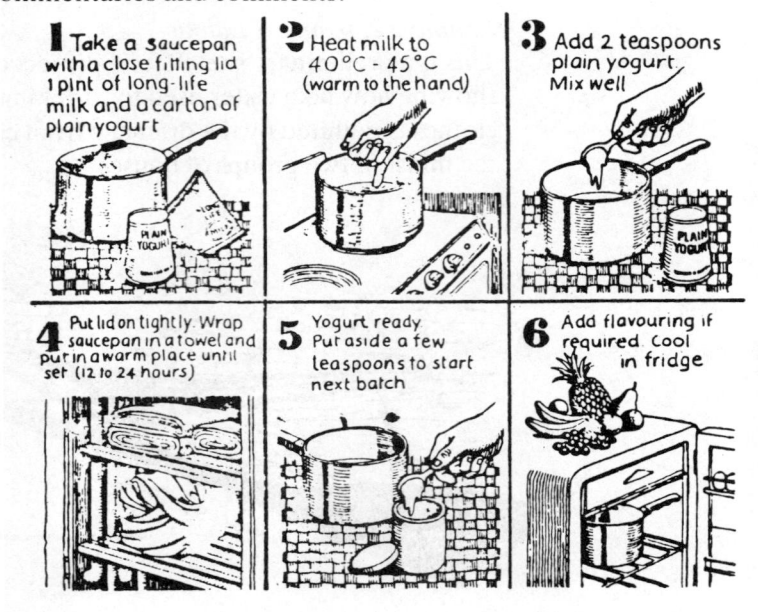

Examples 5 (below) and 6 (on page 156): from Malaysia
These deal with political and economic situations, the first with pollution and the environment and the second with malnutrition and starvation.

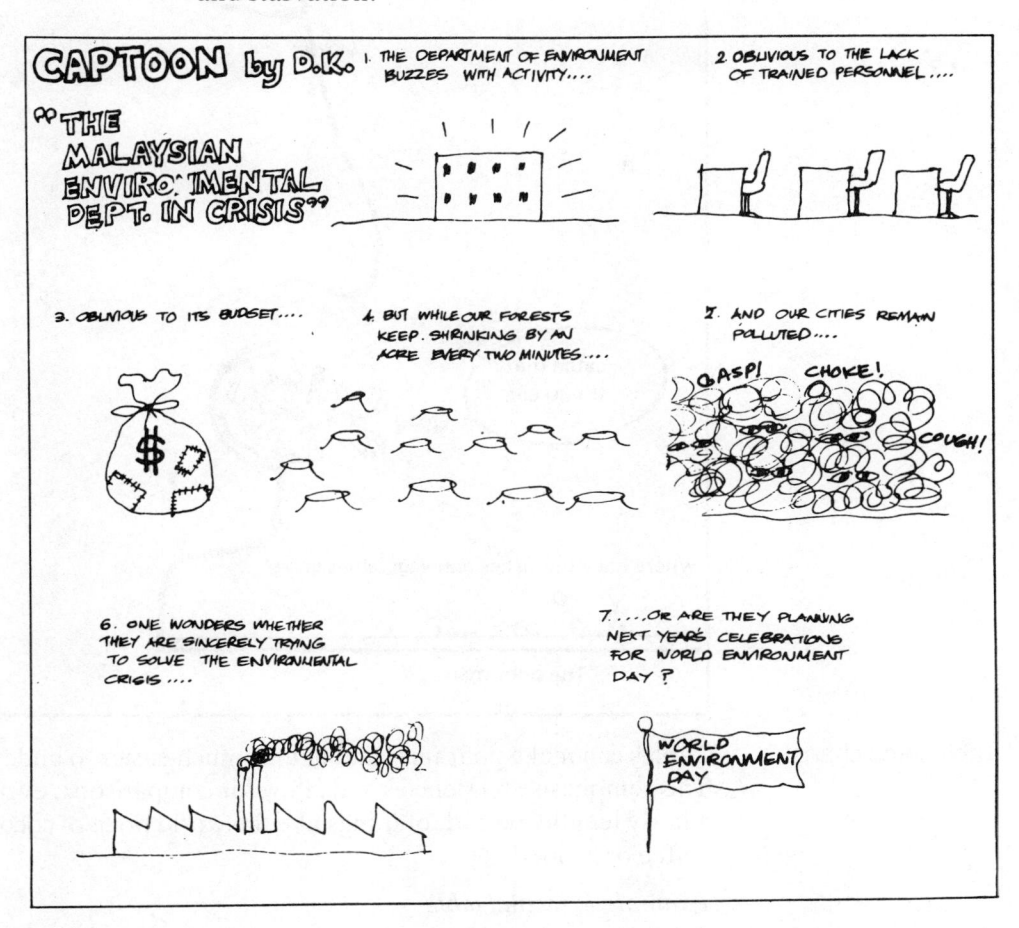

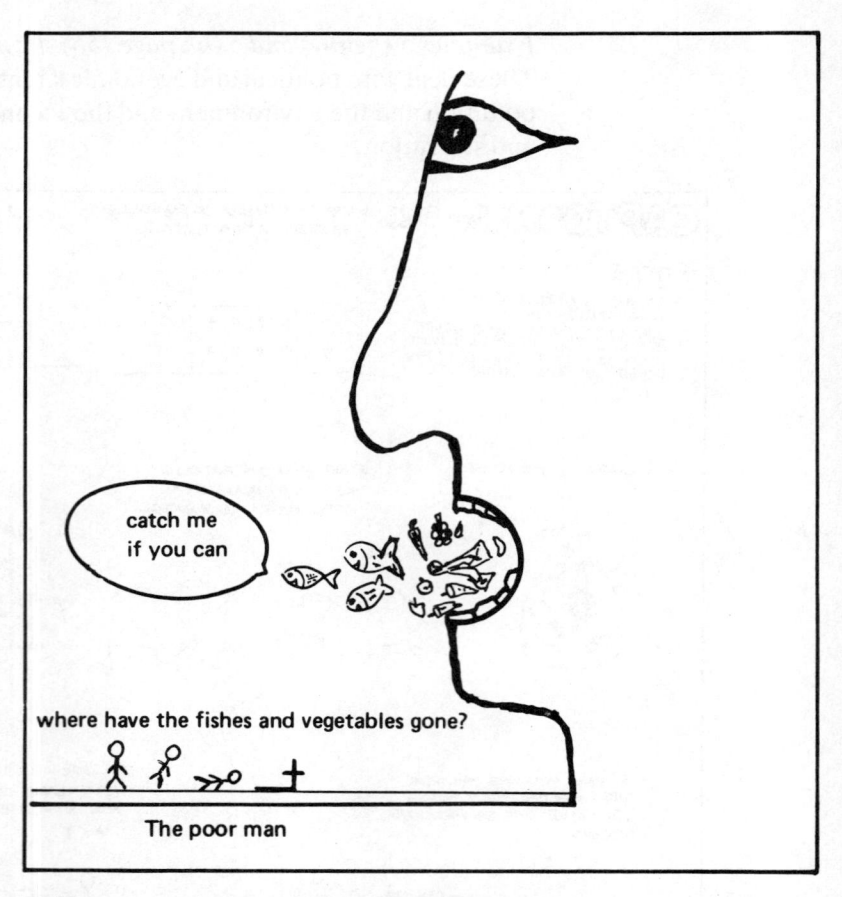

Tables and charts

Tables can make your facts and figures much easier to understand. They emphasise tendencies and allow for comparisons, even over a fairly lengthy period, of things like the world price of cocoa, coffee or rubber.

Example 1: factual table

Some tables concentrate on recording straight facts like accident statistics, unemployment figures – or the average expenditure on insurance, featured in *Money Management Review* no 8.

Average annual expenditure of households with some expenditure in the category of insurance stated 1977 — 1981							Percentage of households with some insurance expenditure	
1977 £	1978 £	1979 £	1980 £	1981 £		1980 %	1981 %
50.6	59.9	71.8	83.2	96.3	Motor insurance	56.4	58.1
15.2	17.6	21.5	28.2	37.7	Insurance of structure	53.1	52.3
9.9	12.5	15.8	21.2	25.8	Insurance of contents	74.5	76.5
	76.9	90.7	97.8	116.7	Medical insurance	3.6	4.5
112.3	130.1	139.9	158.2	183.2	Life assurance	76.5	76.4
13.4	17.8	22.3	22.3	27.2	Other insurance	6.8	7.3

Example 2: rating table

Other tables record people's opinions and preferences. Some kind of a rating system is needed here, such as a five point scale (from excellent to very poor) where the more stars or blobs a product or service notches up the better. The example below, on the suitability of holidays in Britain for different age groups, shows how easy this system is to understand since it gives an instant impression of preferences.

KEY. The more +++, the better

	for families with young children	for teenagers	for young adults	for older people	for a relaxing holiday	for an energetic holiday	for good food	for historical and cultural interest
ENGLAND								
NORTHUMBRIA	++	++	+	++	++	+++	+	+++
LAKE DISTRICT	+	+++	+++	++	++	+++	++	+
YORKSHIRE	++	+++	++	+	++	++	++	++
NORTH WEST	+++	+++	+	++	+	+	++	+
EAST MIDLANDS	+	++	+	+	+	+	+	+
WEST MIDLANDS	+	+++	+++	+++	+++	+	+++	+
EAST ANGLIA	+++	+++	+	+	++	+	+	+
THAMES & CHILTERNS	+	+++	++	+++	++	+	++	+++
WEST COUNTRY including	++	++	+	++	+++	+	++	+
DEVON	++	++	+	++	+++	+	++	+
CORNWALL	++	++	+	+	+++	+	++	+

Examples 3 and 4: bar charts

Charts help if it is particularly important for numbers to make an impact. The example at the top of page 158 is a column chart produced by an environmental studies group to show the success rate of onion sets. They found in their sample D, which is – at a glance – seen to be much worse than the others, that the high proportion of nonstarting onions happened because they bought some of last year's cheap. Note that in their chart the columns are all of the same height, built up in this case of success and failure, to equal 100%. Charts can also be set horizontally. In the example of clothing imports, young people 'borrowed' a similar kind of chart.

157

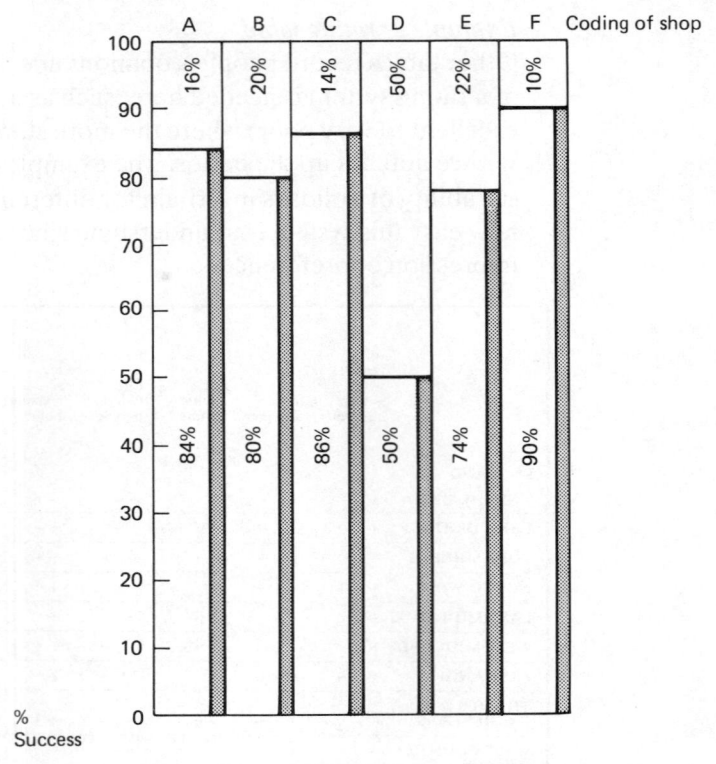

	A	B	C	D	E	F	Coding of shop
top	16%	20%	14%	50%	22%	10%	
bottom	84%	80%	86%	50%	74%	90%	

% Success

Column graph showing growth of instant onions

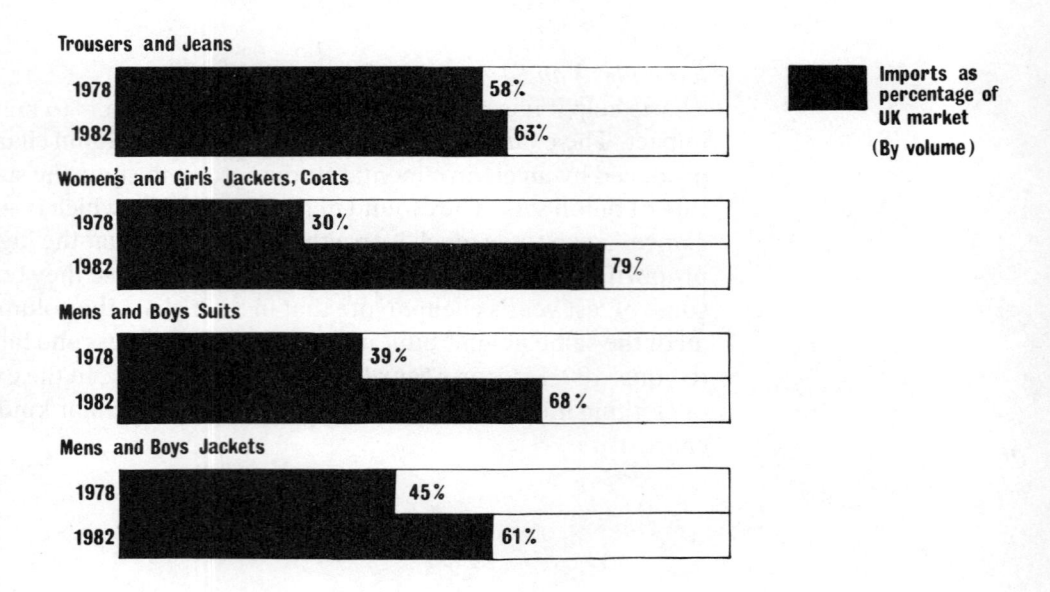

Trousers and Jeans
- 1978: 58%
- 1982: 63%

Women's and Girls Jackets, Coats
- 1978: 30%
- 1982: 79%

Mens and Boys Suits
- 1978: 39%
- 1982: 68%

Mens and Boys Jackets
- 1978: 45%
- 1982: 61%

Imports as percentage of UK market (By volume)

Examples 5 and 6: perspective charts
Such charts can be made more artistic (though aesthetics are less important than accuracy) by using perspective, as in this example which compares the combined populations of Europe in the European Community with those of Russia, China and America. If there is a big difference between the smallest and the largest numbers, then the largest may have to be represented by a 'broken' column.

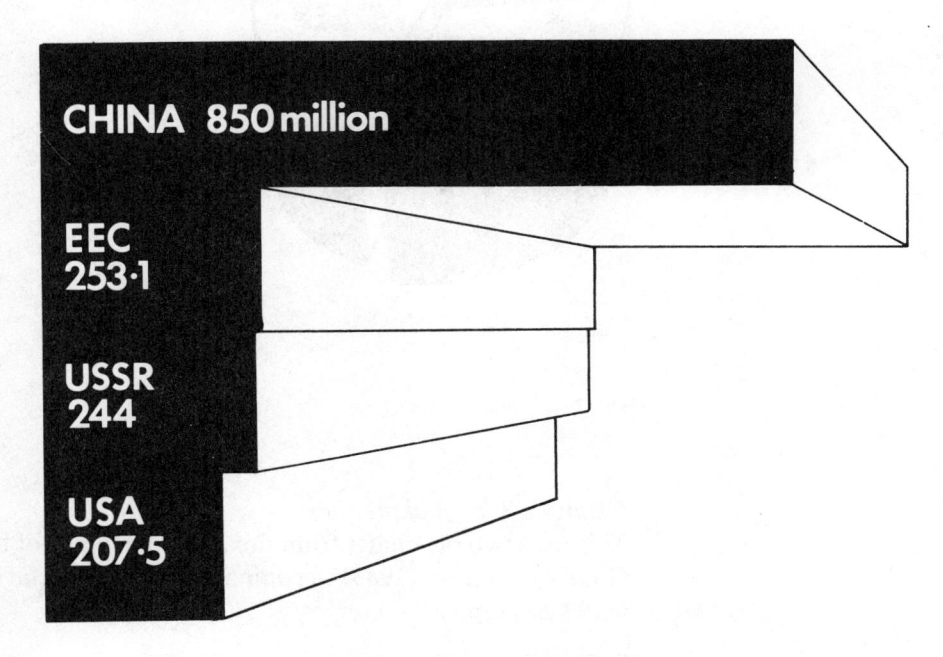

CHINA 850 million

EEC 253·1

USSR 244

USA 207·5

Costs per pupil per year in England 1979/80

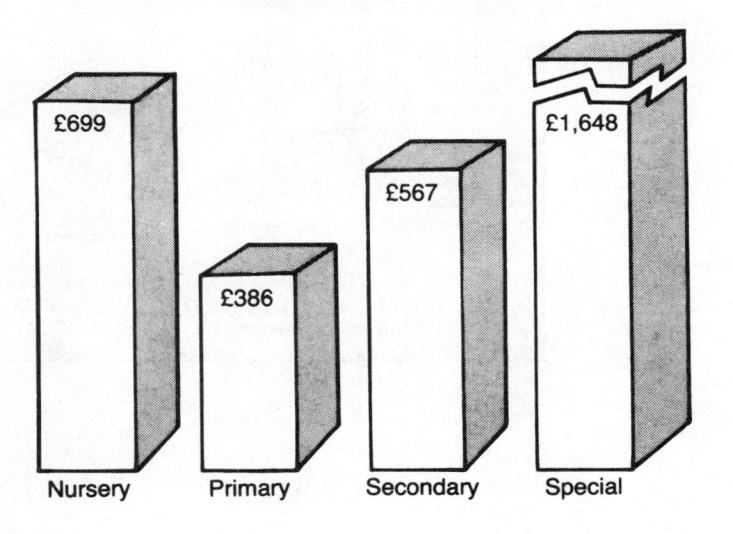

£699 — Nursery
£386 — Primary
£567 — Secondary
£1,648 — Special

Example 7: illustrative pie chart
Pie charts actually look like a pie or cake cut up into slices. This illustration uses perspective to bring home this analogy, showing how young people's time is roughly split into three.

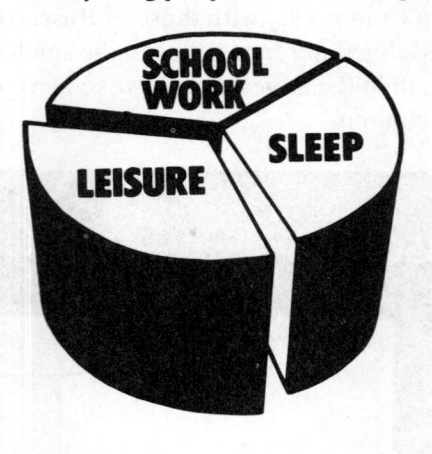

Example 8: factual pie chart
This uses two pie charts from the Annual Report of the British Gas Corporation (1983) to compare the commercial sales of gas with sales ten years later.

Commercial gas sales — Percentage distribution

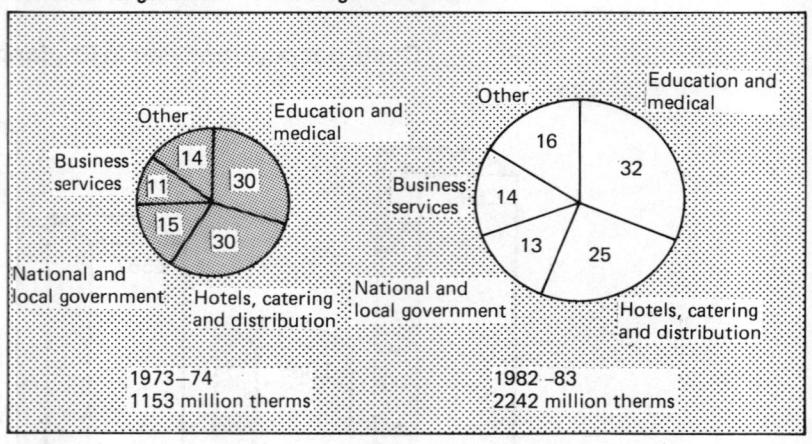

1973–74
1153 million therms

- Other: 14
- Education and medical: 30
- Business services: 11
- National and local government: 15
- Hotels, catering and distribution: 30

1982–83
2242 million therms

- Other: 16
- Education and medical: 32
- Business services: 14
- National and local government: 13
- Hotels, catering and distribution: 25

Example 9: half pie chart
On the other hand a half pie chart was used by the students of the Collège Hohberg in Strasbourg to indicate the cost of books. stationery and clothes at the start of the school year, in a feature published by *Les Dernières Nouvelles d'Alsace*.

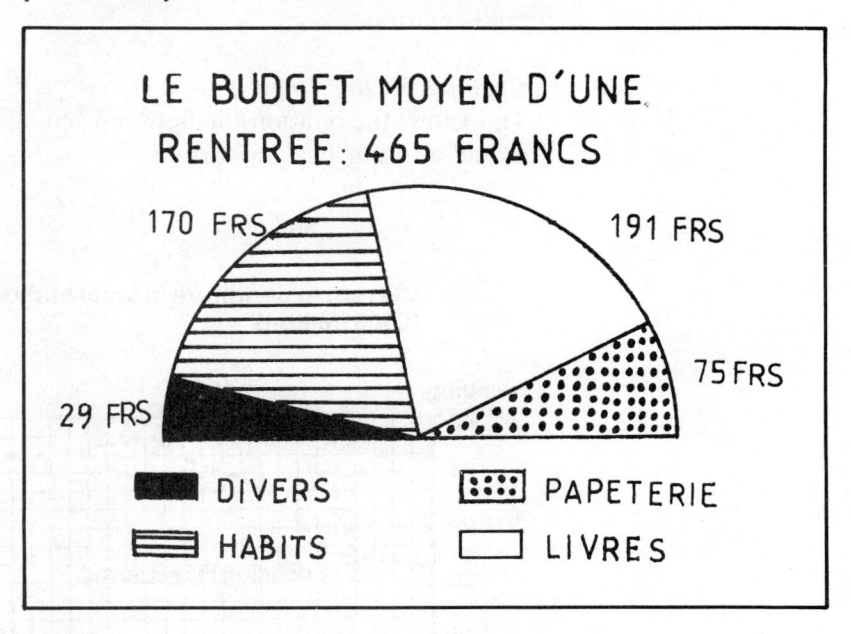

LE BUDGET MOYEN D'UNE RENTREE: 465 FRANCS

170 FRS 191 FRS
29 FRS 75 FRS

■ DIVERS ⁚⁚⁚ PAPETERIE
≡ HABITS □ LIVRES

Accurate pie charts can be hard to draw because not everyone owns, or turns up to class with, a pair of compasses, a sharp pencil and a protractor, and a jam jar or plastic pot does not always produce a good drawing. For, though students can reasonably accurately divide a circle into halves and quarters, it is impossible for anyone to 'cut' a 50° slice by eye alone. Moreover, some lower ability students aren't necessarily aware of the relationship between degrees, percentages, and even fractions. Try them out with a simple example taken from the column chart on 'instant' onions. Sample B had a failure rate of 20% and its pie slice would be $20/100 \times 360° = 72°$; however, sample A gives recording problems since its failure rate works out at 57.6°, and small amounts cannot easily be recorded on a pie chart. As part of a general policy 0.6 could be rounded up, but the problem becomes more acute when your students need to represent less than 5°; it is best to suggest a bar chart in this case as well as when there are a lot of slices in the pie. A large pie, of the retail price index for example, can show within each slice – of food, alcohol, fuel, housing, transport and so on – the main things included.

Line graphs are useful for showing changes over a certain length of time. One school's daily task is to consult the *Financial*

Times so that it can plot the fluctuations of the controversial Britoil share index. Such graphs, using systems of solid, dotted or hyphenated lines, or coloured and shaded bands, provide immediate visual comparisons of subjects such as men and women in full time employment, or boys and girls studying O level mathematics.

Example 10: line graph
This shows the relationship between actual spending and spending in real terms in local authorities.

Current expenditure in local authorities (£000 million)

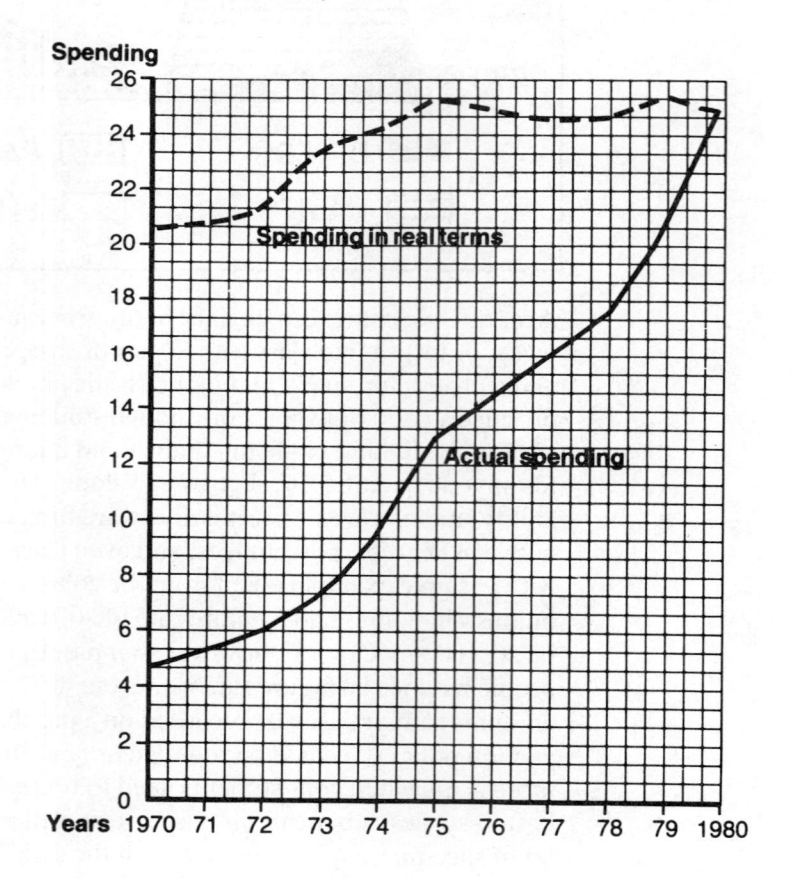

Spending in real terms

Actual spending

Years 1970 71 72 73 74 75 76 77 78 79 1980

Doing graphs as part of a project leads students on to look at other people's graphs more closely, particularly those used in commercial promotions to show financial performance. They realise that starting and cut-off points can be chosen to distort figures by showing the most favourable time span.

All kinds of graphs lend themselves to artistry, appropriate inventiveness, and even to fantasy:

Example 11: pictorial line graph
This shows postal efficiency in Japan, Hong Kong, Malaysia, Thailand and the Philippines, and is reproduced by the Selangor Consumers' Association.

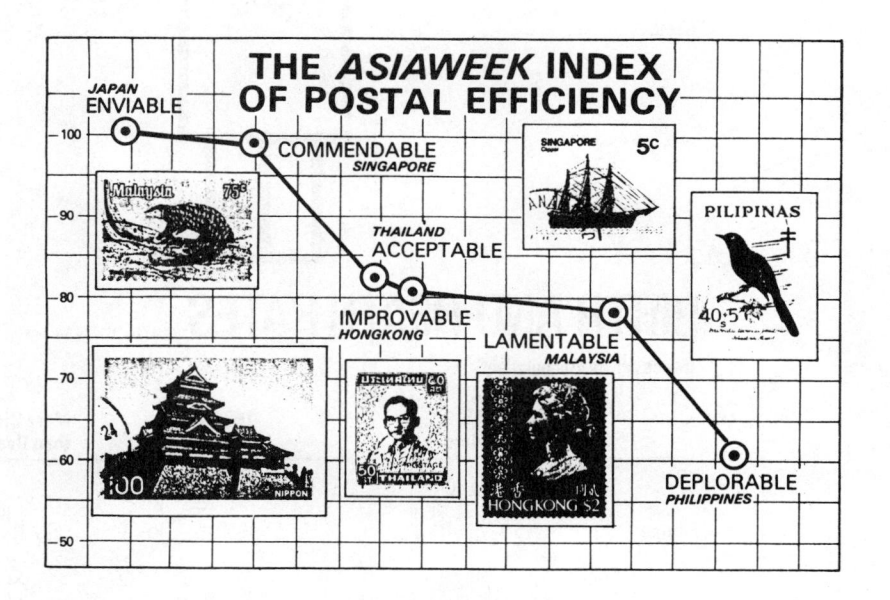

Pictographs are often used to illustrate statistics about people, with little human beings drawn to represent a certain number:

Examples 12 and 13: pictographs
To mark International Year of the Child, the United Nations produced 'humanised' tables to show the number of children born to each woman and birth and death rates.

CHILDREN BORN PER WOMAN

	1970-75	1995-2000
North America	2.19	2.13
Europe	2.28	2.21
USSR	2.42	2.46
Oceania	3.44	2.95
East Asia	3.59	2.26
Latin America	5.27	3.90
South Asia	6.13	4.28
Africa	6.38	5.43

Source: United Nations

BIRTH AND DEATH RATES

Source: United Nations

(Rates per 1000 population)

	1970-75 Birth Rate	1970-75 Death Rate	More Births than Deaths
Europe	16.1	10.4	5.7
North America	16.5	9.3	7.2
USSR	17.8	7.9	9.9
Oceania	24.7	9.4	15.3
East Asia	26.0	9.8	16.2
Latin America	36.7	9.2	27.5
South Asia	42.7	16.8	25.9
Africa	46.5	20.0	26.5

Revision

When your students have finally compounded their facts, findings and illustrations into some sort of edited order, it is a good idea for them to set this draft aside for a few days so that they can look at it with fresh insight. They are likely to be able to do this in any case at school because of the structure of the timetable, but it is worth pointing out that when working they ought to allow for a break. Then they must:

- read through the report as a whole, just as an examiner would
- consider whether each part follows through the original aims, whether anything has been left out, repeated or needs cross referencing, and whether the overall balance is correct
- check the final suitability of the title and subtitle
- check the contents page and its numbering
- verify the text and the illustrations yet again before writing (always with same coloured ink), or typing, the final version – which in turn will have to be gone through to spot a new crop of mistakes
- examine spelling, grammar, punctuation, numbers and references and see that the style is consistent
- write their name clearly on the front cover

Making the most of the results

It's all too easy for an organisation, let alone a school or individual student, to put a large amount of effort into producing a well researched report, and then in exhausted apathy neither follow through its recommendations nor press on with further action. Schools may not feel – or be allowed to feel – that it is part of their function to influence, to campaign or to seek for change; there may simply not be time or opportunity. So, a clearly presented project neatly written up to please the examiner and get a good grade for the student – is that the total aim of a project? Is that always enough? Certainly, it may be all that is possible for an individual project, but group activities can be another matter: here there is the force of a corporate, sometimes indignant view, putting forward conclusions and proposing recommendations; here there is a more varied range of supportive research techniques, and a greater likelihood of involvement with the community if a survey has already been carried out as part of the project. What can be done to take things further than the exam board? Is education indeed neutral? *Should* it be neutral? The question is asked – not in an industrialised but in a *developing* country – with enormous implications about commitment and involvement in all societies. The example on page 166 from Malaysia calls for an answer.

> A project to build a new dam has been announced. Pressure groups make a press statement regarding the consequences of building the dam: displacement of the communities of simple people and destruction of a large number of rare species of fishes etc.
>
> **Whose side would you like to be?**
>
> Why? Do you think you'll be penalised if you take the side of the pressure group?
>
> If the truth is on the side of the pressure groups will you join the group? If not, why? Are you afraid or you don't care? If you are afraid who/what has caused this fear to develop?

> **Is education neutral?**
>
> Take the above case. Even if the pressure group is on the right there will be a lot of people who would not want to get involved. Can it be said that somewhere in the formal education process they have been overtly or covertly cautioned against taking a stand on issues that 'rocks the boat', on issues that clashes with huge power structures?

Getting involved with the press

Stephen: The paper was the biggest thing because all my mates were talking about it, saying 'Oh you was in the paper.'

Luke: Yeah, but did they read it and see what we were on about?

Stephen: Yeah, they all knew what I was on about.

Not all projects result in the coverage that Stephen, Luke and their group enjoyed through their work with travellers. It was a moment of glory that they will probably never again experience.

CIRCUIT DE LA BÊTE DE BOUCHERIE.

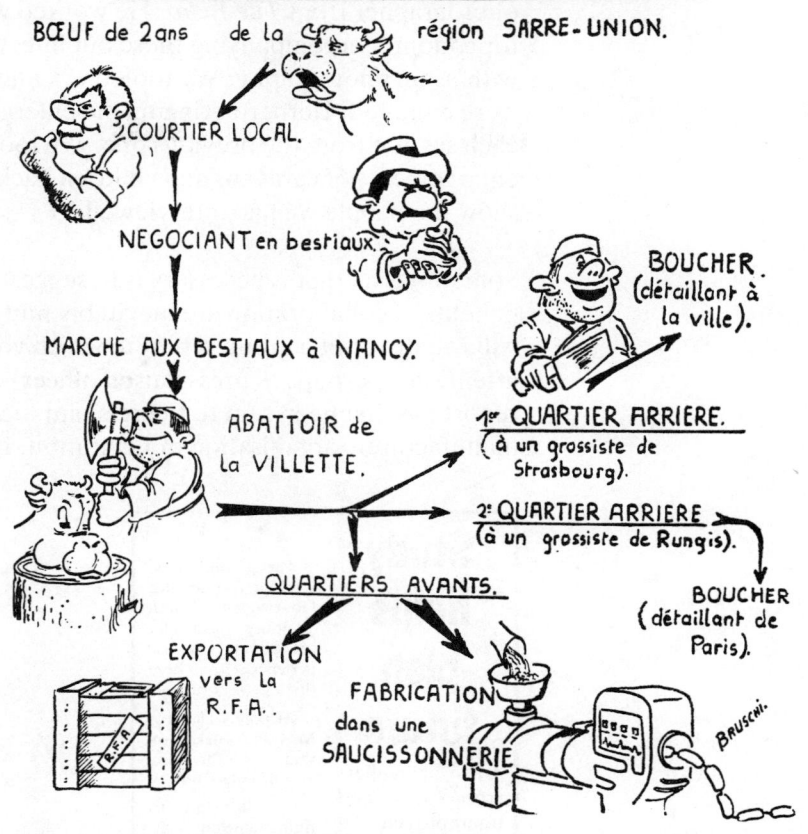

BŒUF de 2 ans de la région SARRE-UNION.

COURTIER LOCAL.

NEGOCIANT en bestiaux.

MARCHÉ AUX BESTIAUX à NANCY.

ABATTOIR de la VILLETTE.

BOUCHER (détaillant à la ville).

1ᵉʳ QUARTIER ARRIERE. (à un grossiste de Strasbourg).

2ᵉ QUARTIER ARRIERE (à un grossiste de Rungis).

BOUCHER (détaillant de Paris).

QUARTIERS AVANTS.

EXPORTATION vers la R.F.A.

FABRICATION dans une SAUCISSONNERIE

In this case contact with the press was deliberately sought by staff and carefully controlled, being regarded as a desirable outcome of the boys' project. But there are many schools who are not in touch with the press, apart from drawing its attention to exam and sports successes: they see it as a seeker out of scandals about sex, drugs and corporal punishment, especially when other local news is in short supply. Others, however, see a newspaper as the means of linking school and community and of providing publicity for promoting a cause. The outstanding European example of regular collaboration is that of the Collège Hohberg and *Les Dernières Nouvelles d'Alsace.* Though it is unusual to have such a large spread – the students' study 'From beef to sausages' appeared in an eight page supplement – it is not unusual for newspapers to make opportunities available: arranging a safety quiz, organising a competition for ideas and inventions designed to improve the community, allowing students to take over promotion and advertising for a day and provide copy and layout for a two page spread, or allocating a reporter to work with a group on a social education project:

'In the winter term we had the services of Bernard Mitchell, a photographer from *The Echo*. He worked with us every session for a month, accompanying those out interviewing, and working with us on photography. We took black and white prints, which were enlarged, Bernard bringing the enlargements back to us each session from the previous one. We took some of these enlargements of caravans and children back the following week to show the people we had interviewed.'

Sometimes all that is necessary is to suggest and ask, since the benefits of collaboration are inevitably mutual. Local newspapers will usually print a group report to which you have drawn attention – perhaps as press liaison officer – especially when the report has first been sent to the relevant local authority, manufacturer, organisation or institution. Local issues such as the

Study helps plan future

AIR travellers from Luton and unemployed local youngsters are both set for brighter horizons thanks to the airport.

School leavers are currently engaged in research work to improve LIA facilities.

About half-a-dozen teenagers canvass up to a thousand travellers per day as they pass through the airport.

The customers were asked their likes and dislikes about the airport, their home bases, destinations and method of reaching the airport.

These and other questions will all help the airport authority mould their facilities to suit demands.

The youngsters, working as part of a Government Youth Training Scheme, are gaining vital experience to help them get a job.

Airport Director Mr Bob Easterbrook said of the six-month-long study:

"It will help us to find out what is attractive about the airport and what is not.

"We are conscious that we cannot be perfect and only the public can tell us how to improve."

Mr Easterbrook expected, at the end of the survey, to have a mass of information to collate.

168

EVERYBODY KNOWS HOW ATROCIOUS THE PUBLIC TRANSPORT IN PENANG IS!

The Georgetown Secondary School Consumers' Society decided to do something about it. The members decided to conduct an initial survey of the problem.

The routes in the Georgetown area covered by the town's five main bus companies formed the area under the survey.

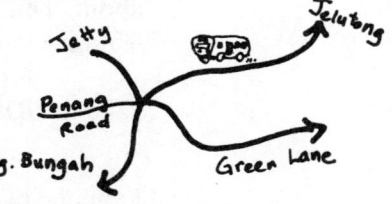

Two main aspects were covered:

1. The bus frequency — on a typical weekday, at peak hours of 6-10 a.m. and 4-8 p.m.
2. The bus-stops — number of stops along a route, conditions of bus-stops, spacing between bus-stops, positions of convenience to commuters.

inadequacy of local transport or leisure facilities, lack of hygiene in cafés and snack bars, inaccuracy of supermarket checkout slips – issues where someone or something (particularly a bureaucracy) seems to be under attack – make popular reading. Or revelations about what people think: should shops be open on Sundays, Crown post offices closed on Saturdays, the Rickmansworth gas showroom shut down for ever? What are conditions like in employment offices? Are appointments systems at the doctor's surgery a good idea? Should dogs be banned from playgrounds? In any school involvement it is important to make sure that your school is accurately identified and a decision taken about mentioning individual pupils: Stephen, Luke and their group were named, and it is the agreed policy of the Collège Hohberg to publish with each section the names of the students and the teacher who worked with them. The reason in both of these cases

---

Enquête réalisée par la classe de 3e 1 du collège Hohberg.

Texte et illustration :
Valérie Barthel, Christiane Nussbaumer, Anne-Marie Boeckel, Hélène Oesterlé, Gilles Burckel, Gérald Schmidt, Marc Diem, Fabienne Spisser, Nicolas Martin, Anne Umecker, Antoine Monge, François Wittersheim, sous la direction de M. Spisser, professeur d'histoire-géographie.

was that a mention in the press provided motivation and therefore raised the standard of the work produced.

There should be clear understanding too about students' own initiatives with the press: approval must first be given before any comments on work at school or college are passed on. But students do have the right, and it is a right that should be encouraged, to write to the papers on an issue they feel strongly about. This is an example of a Penang student writing to *The Star* – but deciding not to disclose his name:

Pupils who are at the mercy of the public transport system

I am one of those unlucky ones who have to depend on the public bus to get to school, and am often late through no fault of mine. This means a fine of 20 cents and getting your name in the prefects' black book.

I'm usually at the bus stop at 7 a.m. though classes start only at 7.45 a.m. One morning I was at the bus stop as usual and at 7.10 the bus which passes my school (route 7) came along. It did not stop because it was already crowded. So I waited hoping that a Sri Negara bus would pass soon (the next route 7 bus would come by only at 7.40).

Finally, at 7.35 a Sri Negara bus which had only a handful of passengers came along. It was behind a route 9 bus which stopped at the bus stop. A lady and I waved to the driver but he purposely drove off. I am sure he saw us and he could have stopped behind the route 9 bus. I am so angry with him and am sorry I forgot to note down the number of that bus. I walked home, knowing that I would be more than a lesson late.

Such correspondence and reaction to it can spark off ideas for school projects with a high degree of motivation.

Working with radio and television	Again, schools can have the same reservation as they have in dealing with the press – the fear of scandal, sensationalism and, in the case of television, the more realistic fear of disruption. Nevertheless, the extension of local radio and television is linking school and community to a much greater extent, not only in the United Kingdom but particularly in countries like Australia where distances are great and the maintenance of communications is an essential part of social and economic existence. Young people are learning to participate, to ask questions, to extend the interviewing skills learned in carrying out surveys into interviewing on radio. It can be quite disconcerting for an adult,

unprepared for such skills, to be interviewed – at Queensland's 4ZZZ FM station, for example – by young people who have researched their subject well, whether on hobbies or junk foods, nationalisation or nuclear power, and who remain doggedly persistent and perceptive in their questioning. For the less confident student who still wants to have a go at broadcasting, the American Consumers' Union circulates scripts to schools which can be practised and taped first, like this example of a report on a consumer fair in the Bronx:

Report to Consumers

You're never too young to learn how to be an alert consumer. That was the message delivered by kids at PS 95 in the Bronx earlier this spring. I'm . . . and this is *Report to consumers*.

The 4th, 5th and 6th graders held a consumer fair in cooperation with Consumers' Union and Fordham Learning Center through a partial grant from the federal government. The fair was part of a special project designed to teach urban minority youngsters basic consumer skills and concepts.

The fair included exhibits by the children of special consumer projects they developed and researched. For instance, one class conducted tests of facial tissues; another did taste tests of different brands of pretzels; and a third did an exposé of the sugar in breakfast cereals. Some of the youngsters explained unit pricing by presenting a comparison shopping exhibit that dramatized the price differences among various brands of a product.

One class showed particular interest in toys advertised on TV. The students devised a product rating system for the toys and then wrote to manufacturers to voice their findings. Another group showed how recycling could be fun. They turned worn-out jeans into jean bookbags, and made piggy banks from gallon bleach bottles and flower arrangements from egg cartons.

A look at some other ways kids learn about consumerism in our next report. This has been *Report to consumers*, and this is . . . signing off.

Fortunately, the mystique of machinery no longer exists, and many young people grow up knowing how to handle complex recording equipment. There is no reason why a radio or video tape should not play its part in providing evidence to support the theme of a project on bad housing, for example, high pressure salesmanship, the handicap of being old, or vandalism. Students working with the Watford Social Education Project did in fact produce video films on the last two items of this list. In one of the student's own words: 'The film was about an old lady who was never visited – the title was called "The death of a neglected old lady". The story was about an old lady, Mrs Smith and her family (the daughter of the old lady and her husband and the three children). Other people in the film are the milkman, the health inspector and an old lady who lives over the street. Also Mrs Smith's daughter has a friend who stops the daughter from going to see Mrs Smith. The film was shot in Holywell Road in Watford, and one shot was taken at a phone box near Watford Football Club.'

The second video film was called 'Vandal'. They scripted the tape as a group while sitting round a large table, and selected their director, cameraman and main star by secret ballot. They had the technical assistance of a student from the London Polytechnic, who allowed the pupils full control of equipment but was available for advice. The first day of shooting took place at the probation office where the boys (some of whom were on probation themselves) were able to demonstrate their full capabilities when they were really interested in a subject. Onlookers were surprised at the skills in cooperation and leadership shown by previously disruptive boys. The boy chosen for director kept control, but managed to lead in fairly democratic style. He also made a point of including five Pakistani boys who had always been excluded by the others, suggesting that they should be in the gang being filmed.

Any participation in broadcasting should be valued only for the opportunities it brings of learning and applying skills and of being an active and involved element in the community. You won't ever make much money out of it, and you may have additional expenses or even inconveniences. Find out first what is expected of you and your students, particularly if an outside camera crew propose to film at your school.

Publishing in schools

The production of *Souvenir* was unusual since schools and colleges do not normally have the resources to create materials for the public. There is the occasional circulation of duplicated sheets – for example, a list of shops and organisations offering special concessions to old people and sent round to day centres and Darby and Joan clubs – but the most that schools usually produce is a prospectus and a magazine. The first can become more useful to parents if it is amplified by student research – for example, by a sixth form social science inquiry into what children in their first secondary year think about their move from primary school. The second can be livened up by printing popular versions of relevant projects – on school meals, uniforms, the cost of getting to school, sports facilities and sex discrimination – and it can also be used to distribute questionnaires: the record questionnaire in chapter 4 was sent out in a number of different school magazines and brought an above average response rate.

It is important to be aware that school publications are subject to libel laws even if they aren't actually sold: the defence is that a report is free from malice and that what it says is true. This is another opportunity for driving home the importance of accuracy and verification.

Demonstrating and displaying

In a long, rather grim, straight corridor there are bright wall dislays designed by fifteen-year-olds, catching the eye and arousing the envy of younger pupils. The exhibition changes from showing the development of cabbage to choucroute, to the effects

Younger children contemplating the winning projects in a competition on energy education

of large farms on village life, to the impact of tobacco growing as a new industry on the inhabitants of Alsace, the use of alternative fuels or the degree of insulation in homes. Other displays or open days are intended to attract and inform parents, and to draw in local people to see what is going on in their school. These events can be part of the school's own calendar or tied in with some other regional, national or even international occasion. Students in Penang, for example, participated in projects intended for an exhibition on consumer complaints and the law. The best project, by Bukit Mertajam High School, showed the dangers and effects

173

Chinese students in Hong Kong taking part in a quiz to celebrate Human Rights Day

of using pesticides on plants and animals and the results of interviews with farmers and smallholders on their observations about ill effects. In Jamaica, schools contribute annually to National Consumer Education Week, producing exhibits on food, safety, health, hygiene, providing a fashion show of traditional clothes, reviving former crafts, competing in a quiz on nutrition, and encouraging self-sufficiency – how to keep a rabbit and make use of every bit of the animal, or how to grow things best suited to soil and family needs. Other schools in other countries participate in parallel events or commemorate particular days such as those for World Food, Environment, Human Rights and Literacy Day. There are also years to celebrate – International Year of the Child, of Women, of the Disabled, and in 1985 of Young People. Participation in such events can help to provide motivation, a target to aim at, and a feeling of solidarity with like minded people in other parts of the world.

Working with other people

Students in the Hertfordshire social education project liked their community service work with the handicapped, the elderly and the gypsies because they had the freedom to escape from the constraints of school. In their own words:

Robert: We've had a good time and we've had responsibilities put upon us.
Duncan: It's just a laugh getting out of school.

Robert: I think we've been given responsibilities we wouldn't have had if we'd stayed in school.
Stephen: If we was in school we would have got nowhere.
Rebecca: We wouldn't have put so much interest in it because we come round here to do something. You wouldn't be interested in it if you was at school, though.
Angela: You'd be in the same old surroundings.
Stephen: We must want to come here because you don't get many people hopping off.
Duncan: They wouldn't want to do it in school, they'd want to come here because you don't get any people in authority do you?
Robert: It's only because there's no authority here and Steve's a good bloke and he's not like our teachers who push us into things.
Stephen: But we must want to come here because there's not many people hop off this.

Adults who are not parents, teachers or potential employers – 'Steve's a good bloke' – have a kind of neutrality about them which makes them more acceptable even to reluctant students. 'To get anything off the ground I think we needed more help from the sort of, you know the older people, you know the people that *do know* about it', says Angela. It can happen that students are also content to work directly with an independent voluntary organisation where people are seen to be doing something for an apparent nothing and to believe in causes to be fought for. It is useful, then, for schools to have a list of organisations where aid can be reciprocal: consumer organisations throughout the world, especially those with a network like the National Federation of Consumer Groups in Britain, are likely to be able to give practical help on specific projects, and to welcome, in return, access to a labour force. Schools can help in carrying out surveys either by completing relevant questionnaires or by actively taking part in distribution, interviewing or collation of results; they can observe, record and check. This kind of collaboration, provided the timing and choice of subject is right, can lead on to a project which satisfies the requirements of school, examiners, community – and students.

In Malaysia, cooperation with consumer groups has led to the setting up of consumer clubs in much the same way as British schools might have a stamp or chess club. They are very project orientated, motivated by the fact that correct information, knowledge of the law, the art of choosing carefully and critically, all help to make the most of scant resources. Some of the investigations are forcefully controversial: what goes into rubbish bins? Which is the best buy in sanitary towels? If publicity for a school is undesirable, then collaboration with a consumer organisation can divert its main thrust. Other appropriate organisations, which vary from area to area and country to country, include environment and conservation groups, literacy, education and advice agencies, housing, welfare and women's organisations, which have as their hallmark both action and involvement. They can offer the opportunity for participation, the promotion and publicity of ideas produced by projects. The search for areas of common interest, the joining of forces with such organisations, the need for accuracy, patience, tolerance, dedication, is not just mutually beneficial: it is education in its positive form. Here education is not neutral, it is committed.

START IN A SMALL WAY ....

This book has provided many examples of project based contributions, some large and some small, some immensely time consuming and others almost instant, but all of them real. There is nothing too humble to consider as a starting point for involvement.

6 Conclusions and reflections

Chapters 4 and 5 show teachers in a new light, learning techniques which previously would have been regarded as somebody else's job. Market resarchers carry out surveys – finding out how people are likely to vote or what they think about the latest packeted pie – not teachers or lecturers! Not so: investigative learning needs the understanding and implementation of at least some of the skills of commercial researchers, interviewers, social workers, organisers, administrators, statisticians, reporters, journalists and so on. The skills of the classroom are now drawn from a vast range of relevant expertise from outside school: this is part of the growing – and more readily recognised – interdependence of school, college, community, occupation and work. So the skills learned at colleges of education, possibly long ago, may have to be amplified and extended, and certainly constantly updated.

The burden of involvement in project work is very heavy. Chapter 1, in 'What is the point of a project?', discussed the crucial question of what is achieved by a project, and subsequent chapters have given guidance – largely through practical examples and suggestions – about the various techniques which can be used in discovery learning. But is it all worth while? Will the Middlesex Polytechnic teacher who 'did a very bad one once' feel reassured enough to take on another project?

Itemising the main problems, coming face to face with them, is one way of diminishing their intensity:

Summary of the problems
Organisation

1   A project can appear within a single subject – CSE mode 3 home economics, commerce or social studies. The first problem here is fighting for a big enough block in the timetable, particularly if out-of-school activities are concerned. The usual 40 minute span is not enough for effective project work. The second problem is that of controlling, guiding and monitoring a classful of students who

are all doing different projects; choice and freedom of action is desirable wherever possible, but there is always going to be someone who doesn't know what to do, which means that there must be a prepared list of suggestions. The third problem lies in possible overlap with other subjects: it is not unknown for students to be cunningly doing the same project on advertising or labelling for different teachers.

2 Projects can be multidisciplinary, and indeed ideally should not be confined to a single subject – variety of approach and input gives an enrichment and a broader base to the final presentation. Yet the organisation of consultation between different departments, let alone embarking on true team teaching, is a daunting prospect at a time when it is difficult enough to find time for routine meetings. Moreover, many schools and colleges are now built in such a way that physical isolation of departments causes mental isolation of staff.

3 If a project is done as a group activity, thus bringing in the interplay of different social skills, there is the problem of organising groups with the minimum of interference yet ensuring a balance of ability and contribution among its members. Remote, unobtrusive control is needed over dominant leaders at one end of the scale and noncontributors at the other.

4 There is the sheer organisational intensity of preparation – of finding time to locate sources of information to provide guidelines for those with little initiative, working out suggestions, arranging groups, planning briefing sessions, duplicating questionnaires and so on. Some of this activity is fortunately 'one off' and, apart from updating, does not have to be started afresh every academic year.

Supervision

1 It is difficult to reconcile freedom to choose subject and method of work with the question of control and even discipline. Projects can involve discussion, debate and even dispute, and they will certainly demand consultation of resources. Who knows whether Peter, who says he is going off to the library to find out about solar power, is really going off for a quick smoke? A teacher who wants silence in the serried rows of desks will not want to embark on the hustle and bustle of a project. Activity is the keyword, and activity is not likely to be silent.

2 What is the role of the teacher here – to be available as a consultant on request, to interfere as little as possible, to act as an umpire? It is very difficult psychologically to be a mere presence, allowing students the freedom to make – and learn

from – their mistakes; educational traditions are against this. Nevertheless, progress has to be watched over, by taking in materials for scrutiny at intervals determined and known well in advance. Detective work will be necessary in recognising chunks that have been copied out from books, and in picking on the cartels that are known to operate among well organised but lazy minded students. Sometimes there is a suspicion of a parental contribution. How well do you know them? How good are they at lying?

3. Many projects require investigations to be carried out away from school and college. The ratio of staff to student can never be big enough, whether in an advisory or in a supervisory capacity. Mishaps occur: what do you do if:

- on a visit to the local sewage works as part of an investigation into refuse disposal, one of your students falls in
- a student slips down the chute at a flour mill while following through the sequence from grain to bread
- another, doing a project on packaging, slips his ballpoint pen into a tray of pork chops on a conveyor belt, which are then wrapped for sale in plastic film
- a group decide to show you their prowess in picking padlocks in a public cycle shed?

If a large scale inquiry is to be carried out with students interviewing the public on their attitudes to half day closing, the sale of council houses or the provision of a new pedestrian precinct, then it is advisable to inform the police in advance. And in the case of school students, the consent of their parents must be asked before they go out of school.

Cost

1. A project implies a result of some sort, ranging from a report, to a diagnosis, to a product. It is as well to bear the expected result in mind before starting off so that original choice takes into account materials available. Paper, coloured pens, folders would be used in more traditional methods of learning, so don't include them in project budgets. If outside activities are part of the project, then plan it on the basis of local inquiries and investigations.
2. Resource materials can sometimes be more of a problem in their availability than in their cost. The difficulty lies in knowing what exists and where to get it in an up-to-date version, but there are excellent free or low cost materials available from banks, post offices, government departments,

insurance offices and companies, and building societies. In general, beware of bias, particularly in commercial publications.

Assessment

1. All projects inside or outside the formal education system need some kind of evaluation and assessment; they may be part of an examination syllabus, they may provide an entry to a competition, or they may be part of an award system like the Duke of Edinburgh's award schemes. The problem is to evolve some kind of measuring scheme which can be seen to be fair.

2. Since each student, or group of students, is likely to be doing a different project, it is difficult to make comparable assessments. Since a project is not like a standardised test, the burden of marking is enormously heavy, but you can lighten it by making a detailed assessment scheme in advance and discussing it with your students, using the following headings:

   - general understanding of the task and the setting out of aims and objectives
   - collection, selection and classification of resource materials
   - preparation and planning of experimental procedures (e.g. carrying out a survey)
   - collation and analysis of results
   - presentation of results
   - conclusions and reflections: what next?

3. If you need to carry out continuous assessment as part of the course, the mark problem can be solved by monitoring achievement at each of these six levels, preferably with two assessors.

4. Since it is not just content of a project which is important, but also the achievement of skills, how does one measure behavioural characteristics – involvement, originality of thought, independence, ability to fit in with a group, and so on? The only person who can have any glimmering of appreciation of change is a teacher or youth leader who has known and had the confidence of a student for a long period and has been able to build up a 'profile'. A grade is easier to provide than a mark.

5. Failure to achieve a result, or failure through a result based on a false premise (as can happen with some comparative testing projects), is not necessarily a useless piece of work. In fact it can have been a very worthwhile activity, but how do you evaluate it? This depends on supervision and *continuous* assessment.

Psychological demands

1 It is difficult to specify your objectives in behavioural terms so that you know in advance where your students are going and when they have arrived.
2 A project is not like other forms of teaching and learning, and it does not necessarily have quantifiable results; there may in fact be no single correct answer or solution, there may be multiple possibilities, or the project may end up pointing in the wrong direction. It is difficult for an orthodox teacher to accept that there will not be an absolute right or wrong, that some things can be learnt though they can't be taught. To what extent does this undermine traditional self-respect?
3 Likewise, in certain projects, it can happen that individual students have greater specific knowledge than the teacher – about microelectronics, car engines or cameras. There has to be a recognition of the interdependence of skills and knowledge – with the teacher retaining supremacy as an experienced organiser and administrator, but tactfully recognising that heavy handed authority can constrain and contaminate the concepts of active learning.

Pros and cons of project based learning

The following is a summary of a discussion with 'Cert Ed' teachers at Middlesex Polytechnic:

For	**Against**
1 Students choose their own subject.	1 Difficulty of controlling and guiding a large number of different projects.
2 Encouragement of a sense of commitment and personal responsibility.	2 Disciplinary problems – difficulty of checking up on what's going on
3 Personal research rather than undertaking a set of exercises with pre-determined answers.	3 Need for detective work – is it original or has it been copied?
4 Personal responsibility for organising time.	4 Difficulty of fitting in project work on the timetable, especially when the activity is multidisciplinary
5 Working together in groups, and in the community.	5 Organisation of different groups and ensuring a fair contribution from each member as well as being aware of the problems
6 Analytical and evaluative approach instead of the traditional recall of facts.	
7 Students remember best what they have found out for themselves.	

8   There is a definite end result.
9   The end result can be used to take the project further to be of advantage to others.
10 Students can start from something that is familiar or that they have had experience of.
11 Students move away from dependence on outside evaluation and set their own standards.
12 Some things can be learnt, though they can't be taught.

of leadership and dominance.
6   Cost of resource materials, supplies and travel.
7   Supervision of out-of-school activities.
8   Difficulties in getting access to the right information.
9   Difficulty in knowing exactly where you are going and when you have got there.
10 No single correct answer exists.
11 Difficulty in assessment.
12 Problem of changing attitudes to accept that there are certain areas where students' knowledge is superior.

The choice then exists – to incorporate projects into existing teaching methods in spite of their difficulties, or to reject this approach. A decision has to be made, for project based learning can no longer be ignored. There is little doubt that the most effective way of learning is to find things out for yourself. As a method of instruction, discovery techniques can create a long lasting impression in the mind of the students. For things they discover for themselves become part of their experience and therefore strengthen self-confidence. With the lecture method of teaching, the chalk and talk of the classroom taking up to 42% of teaching time in the Hatfield Polytechnic survey, the emphasis is on a one way flow of facts during which attention wanders and vital points are missed. Afterwards the amount of information retained will be small. But when students have to find things out for themselves about subjects which interest and concern them, then they make a disciplined analysis of the situation and they retain information longer – perhaps forever. 'Do you remember, Miss, that day we did Peter's dog?' Peter's dog was 'done' more than ten years ago.

Bibliography

Abrahams M *A Short Guide to Social Survey Methods*, National Council for Social Services, 1972
Adamson C *Consumers in Business*, National Consumer Council, 1982
Allen D, Healey M and Millington L *The Way the Money Goes*, BBC, 1978
Assessment techniques in secondary schools, *Secondary School Journal*, November 1979
Atkinson J *A Handbook for Interviewers*, HMSO, 1967
Backstrom C H and Hursh G D *Survey Research*, North Western University Press, Evanston, Illinois, 1963
Barry B and Costigan M *Real Life Maths: Numeracy for Living*, Ashton Scholastic, New South Wales, 1979
Callet P, Seiler G and Spisser M *l'Education du Consommateur*, Scodel, 1981
Chase S and Schlink F *Your Money's Worth*, Macmillan, 1927
Connell W F, Koopman C M and Hoban C A *Studying the Local Community*, George Allen and Unwin, 1978
Consumer Action Activities: a Problem-solving Framework, Washington DC, US Government Printing Office, 1974
Consumer Affairs Bureau, *Consumer Education – an Activity Approach for Schools*, Australian Government Publishing Service, 1982
Consumers' Association, *Consumer Education* – a Resource Handbook for Teachers, Hodder and Stoughton, 1979
Consumers' Association, *The Which? Guide to your Rights*, Hodder and Stoughton, 1980
Consumers' Association of Penang, *Consumer Education – a Comprehensive Reader for Malaysian Secondary Schools*, 1977
Consumers' Institute, *Consumer Education in New Zealand Secondary Schools – a Survey*, 1983

Consumers' Union of the United States Inc, *Penny Power*, six times a year

Dangers and Disasters, HMSO, 1978

De Bono E *Children Solve Problems*, Allen Lane and Penguin, 1972

Dewey J *Democracy and Education*, Macmillan, New York, 1916

Dobinson H M *Basic Skills You Need*, Nelson, 1976

Easen P *Mathematics Across the Curriculum: Problem-based Investigations*, Open University, 1979

Fergus A *Finding out from Books*, Hulton, 1977

French E *Consumer Education – Guidelines for Teachers*, Department of Public and Consumer Affairs, South Australia, 1980

Games and Simulations, BBC, 1972

Gender and the Secondary School Curriculum, Bulletin 6, Equal Opportunities Commission

Green, Hayden D *Consumers in the Economy*, South-Western Publishing, 1983

Godfrey W and Robertson S *Standardised Methods for the Sensory Analysis of Food*, British Standards Institution, 1983

Gordon L J and Lee S M *Economics for Consumers*, van Nostrand, 1977

Hanson W J *Communications*, Longman, 1977

Holley B and Skelton V *Economics Education 14–16*, National Foundation for Educational Research in England and Wales, 1980

Huff D *How to Lie with Statistics*, Pelican, 1978

International Organisation of Consumers' Unions, *Food and Nutrition Resource Pack*, 1982

International Organisation of Consumers' Unions, Regional Office for Asia and the Pacific, *Ideas for Consumer Action*, 1981

International Organisation of Consumers' Unions, *Survey Work*, 1974

Jacobson J and Maccoll P *Real Life Reading: Skills for Functional Literacy*, Ashton Scholastic, New South Wales, 1978

Lawton D *Investigating Society*, Hodder and Stoughton, 1979

Levin L *Human Rights – Questions and Answers*, UNESCO Press, 1981

Life Offices' Association and Associated Scottish Life Offices, *Money Management Review*, termly; also *Spending and Saving: a Pack of Learning Materials*, 1983

Lowndes B *Making News: Producing a Community Newspaper*, National Federation of Community Organisations, 1982

McGraw E *Population Today*, Kaye and Ward, 1979

Marland M *The Craft of the Classroom: Survival Guide*, Heinemann, 1976. See also *Curriculum and Timetable of the Secondary School*
Merrit J E *What Shall we Teach?* Ward Lock International, 1974
Moser C A and Kalton G *Survey Methods in Social Investigation*, Heinemann, 1971
National Consumer Council, *The Fourth Right of Citizenship: a Review of Local Advice Services*, 1979
National Consumer Council, *Consumers and Credit*, 1980
National Consumer Council, *A Better Class of Consumer*, 1983
National Federation of Consumer Groups, *A Handbook of Consumer Law*, Consumers' Association and Hodder & Stoughton, 1983
National Federation of Consumer Groups, *Paper Bag*, 1982
Nelson G *Problems of Design*, Whitney, New York, 1957
Oppenheim A N *Questionnaire Design and Attitude Measurement*, Heinemann, 1966
Paine F A *Packaging and the Law*, Newnes Butterworths, 1973
Papanek V *Design for the Real World*, Granada, 1980
Payne S L B *The Art of Asking Questions*, Studies in Public Opinion no 3, Princeton University Press, 1951
Pouvoir Economique des Consommateurs, Ministre de l'Economie, Paris, 1980
Ridout R and Yglesias J R C *Openings in English*, Hutchinson, 1981
Project Methods in Higher Education, Society for Research into Higher Education, 1975
Project Orientation in Higher Education, Brighton Polytechnic and University Teaching Methods Unit, 1976
Schools Council, *Community Service and the Curriculum*, HMSO, 1968
Selangor Consumers' Association, *The World We Live In – a Closer Look*, 1983
Teaching Statistics 11–16: Statistics in your World, Schools Council, Foulsham Educational, 1980
Slater N *Commerce for the Consumer*, Pitman, 1967
South Hackney School, *The Need to Know – a Community Information Project*, 1979
Trusteeship Foundation Bombay, *Integrated Rural Development Programme*, 1982
Tuck M *How do we Choose? – a Study in Consumer Behaviour*, Methuen, 1976
Williams A *Reading and the Consumer*, Hodder and Stoughton, 1976
Yeomans K A *Statistics for the Social Scientist*, Penguin, 1968

Index

assessment
   record keeping, 25
   marking projects, 35, 178–81
brainstorming, 30–3
   in action, 26, 107
case histories, 10, 121
   examples, 104, 120–3, 127
choice
   subject, 9, 15–17, 24, 84
   motivation/method, 8–10, 23, 52
   preference charts, 34–5
community
   projects, 94–104
   involvement, 9–10, 165, 177
   media and collaboration, 166–71
consumer education, 14–15, 116
   Nordic project, 6, 13
   Karnataka, 19
   labelling and retail trade, 26–8
   CERES, 44
   week in Jamaica, 174
   (*see* developing countries)
consumer organisations
   IOCU, 44, 93, 124
   NFCG, 122, 175
   CA, 5, 7, 23, 46, 54, 58, 65, 69, 80, 90, 120, 148, 154
   RoSPA, 7, 33
   BSI, 48, 82
   HK Consumer Council, 23, 174
   CA Penang, 65, 125, 169, 173
   Consumers' Institute NZ, 65–8, 127
   Consumer unions US, 87, 134, 171
   CA Selangor, 155–6, 163, 166
curriculum, 12, 13, 15, 18–19, 25
design, 3–4, 9, 29–30
developing countries
   Jamaica, 1, 104
   India, 19–20, 25, 69, 104–6
   Malaysia, 69, 116, 124–6, 129–31, 135, 155–6, 165–6
   Kenya, 49, 104–5
   Korea, 69, 153
   Penang, 69, 96, 124–6, 169–70, 177
   Thailand, 92
   Sri Lanka, 153
information
   obtaining facts, 42–3, 45–51, 53
   evaluation, 48–50, 148
keywords, 24–5, 111–13
market research (*see* surveys)
   language, 56–8
   manufacturers and teachers, 88, 177
mass media
   teaching materials, 43–4, 124–6
   role, 8, 97, 123, 127, 134, 168, 170–2
   Asia/Pacific Institute for Broadcasting, 129, 135
motivation, 23, 172, 174–5
   (*see* mass media/choice)
new technology, 10, 12–13, 171
   use of computers, 43, 51, 57, 63

organisation
   of class matrices/charts, 34–5, 37
   of plans, 37, 40, 83, 142
   of report writing, 147
   summary of problems, 177–8
problem solving, 3–4, 6, 29–31, 117
   (*see* brainstorming and case histories)
projects
   definitions, 1–5
   aims and development, 3, 5–10, 36–7
   structuring, 37, 45
   summary, 177–82
   project on safety, 30–48 (passim)
questionnaires
   asking questions, 57–9, 62–5, 72–5
   examples, 58–62
relevance
   importance in education, 6–8
   project work, 8, 19
   examinations, 13, 19
   Nordic project, 6, 13
   importance in NOP, 14
report writing
   titles, 145
   contents, 146
   introduction, 146
   main section, 147–9
   conclusion, 149–50
resources
   consumer resources, 26–8
   libraries, 42
   specific sources, 43–4
   press as a resource, 123–4
   in the classroom, 124–6
   availability, 179–80
role playing
   purpose, 128–9
   examples, 129–31
   case histories, 121–2
skills (*see* social education)
   basic skills, 8–9, 112
   assessment, 180
   Gantt charts, 37–8
   self-management, 40
   communications/survey, 46–8, 53
   critical thinking, 125
social education (*see* community)
   projects, 76–8, 100–3, 171
   community service, 174
   working with press, 167–8, 170
   use of video tapes, 171–2
surveys (*see* market research and questionnaires)
   aims and types, 53–6
   specimens, 65–9
   interviewing, 70–8, 170–1
   recording information, 75–6
testing, 78–92
verification, 148, 169–70